DO DOGS HAVE BELLY BUTTONS?

Do Dogs Have Belly Buttons?
Answers to the 100+ Most Commonly
Asked Canine Questions

Michelle A. Rivera

Adams Media
Avon, Massachusetts

Published by Adams Media, an F+W Publications Company
57 Littlefield Street
Avon, MA 02322
www.adamsmedia.com

ISBN-10: 1-59869-163-5
ISBN-13: 978-1-59869-163-4

Library of Congress Cataloging-in-Publication Data
Rivera, Michelle A.
Do dogs have belly buttons? / Michelle A. Rivera.
p. cm.
ISBN-13: 978-1-59869-163-4 (pbk.)
ISBN-10: 1-59869-163-5 (pbk.)
1. Dog—Miscellanea. I. Title.
SF426.2.R58 2007
636.7—dc22   2007002929

Printed in the United States of America.
J I H G F E D C B A

This publication is designed to provide accurate and authoritative information with regard to the subject matter covered. It is sold with the understanding that the publisher is not engaged in rendering legal, accounting, or other
professional advice. If legal advice or other expert assistance is required, the
services of a competent professional person should be sought.
—From a *Declaration of Principles* jointly adopted by a Committee of the
American Bar Association and a Committee of Publishers and Associations

Many of the designations used by manufacturers and sellers to distinguish
their products are claimed as trademarks. Where those designations appear
in this book and Adams Media was aware of a trademark claim, the designations have been printed with initial capital letters.

This book is available at quantity discounts for bulk purchases.
For information, please call 1-800-289-0963.

*This book is dedicated to
dogs everywhere, especially those
who are hurting.*

CONTENTS

Chapter One

Pooch Parts: How a Dog's Body Works **1**

Chapter Two

Doggy Deeds: Why Dogs Do the Things They Do **17**

Chapter Three

Educated Guesses: Things Dogs Do and Why We Think They Do Them **57**

Chapter Four

Myths, Sayings, and Truths: What We Say and Why We Say 'Em **75**

Chapter Five

Hound Health 97

Chapter Six

Amazing Feats 115

Chapter Seven

FOREWORD

by Susan Helmink
Professor of Animal Sciences and Humane Educator
University of Illinois at Urbana-Champaign

I have a confession to make . . . I have never owned a dog. I have fostered dogs, pet-sat dogs, cared for and trained shelter dogs, helped others train their dogs, and, of course, admired dogs my entire life. This may sound strange coming from someone who teaches classes related to dog selection, care, behavior, and training.

As a child, I did the usual begging for a dog (and a horse), but to no avail. As an adult I have come close to adopting a dog a few times. Working at an animal shelter and studying animal welfare issues, however, has shown me that I am not able to provide the time that a dog deserves. But I do manage to fill my life outside the home with dogs, and this arrangement has worked well for me.

I have bonded with many dogs, and the more I spend time with them, the more I am fascinated by these intelligent, social, and fun-loving creatures. Dogs may have common traits and behaviors, but each one is truly an individual. One only has to take a walk with a dog to begin appreciating this species' special qualities. What can she find so fascinating on the ground? Why is she rolling in that stinky spot? How did she see that rabbit before I did? We are fascinated by dogs because they can do things we cannot. We are amazed when dogs sniff out bombs or drugs, or locate a lost child or an injured person beneath a pile of rubble. Even with the best technology, we cannot equal what dogs can do.

Beyond the physical wonders of dogs, we are equally fascinated by the way dogs can make us feel. Various studies have shown that being in the presence of a friendly dog relaxes us. Children are more comfortable reading to a dog than to their peers or a teacher; thus there are library programs in which a child is sent to a quiet area with a certified dog to practice reading. You are more likely to talk to a stranger if he has a dog with him. Dogs break the ice, making them ideal for programs that allow dogs and their handlers to visit nursing homes. The residents fulfill their need to touch and nurture, and the dogs provide a conversation-starter.

A major concept at play is the nonjudgmental nature of dogs. A dog will never criticize your clothes, your hair, how you live, what kind of car you drive, what you eat. This makes us feel really good about ourselves. We can be completely at ease and not concern ourselves with how we are perceived. We can be silly with dogs; we can share our problems with dogs; we can cuddle with dogs. And due to the social nature of dogs, they are nearly always ready and waiting to interact with us.

At a conference in San Francisco, Ed Sayres (then president of the San Francisco SPCA) talked of his dog doing a dance of excitement as Mr. Sayres got out of bed each morning, as if to say "He's up, he's up!" Mr. Sayres said it was hard not to be in a good mood when you have a dog just bursting with life and ready for whatever the day brings. That is perhaps another reason why we love dogs so much. Their happy mood, their live-life-in-the-moment attitude, is contagious.

When the physical skills of dogs are combined with their feel-good nature, there's a powerful and amazing outcome. Consider guide dogs, hearing dogs, assistance dogs, and therapy dogs. For individuals with physical disabilities, dogs not only provide locomotion or ambulatory skills; they instill self-confidence and companionship.

Dogs can also encourage people to engage in physical therapy. Merely petting a dog may provide physical therapy for a person who has limited abilities to use his hand or arm. People recovering from certain shoulder ailments can toss a ball for a dog to fetch, turning what might be considered boring and painful rehabilitation exercises into a game. Having a dog can give a person recovering from an illness or injury or a person wanting to lose weight the incentive to go for more frequent and longer walks.

There are a host of emotional benefits that go along with these physical benefits, combining into a powerful package we can't seem to get enough of. In *Do Dogs Have Belly Buttons?* Michelle Rivera provides a whimsical look into the lives of these magnificent beings. She provides answers to many questions you have likely thought about, and others that may surprise you. Lighthearted and fun to read, this book also provides a lot of good-to-know information; details that will help us better understand the dogs who share our lives. You may find yourself contemplating the questions with others, or using your newfound knowledge at your next social gathering. Throughout the book Rivera also reminds us of our responsibility to dogs; that we must provide for the needs of our own dogs and be good stewards to companion dogs everywhere who depend on humans for their health and welfare.

A better understanding of dogs and their motivations will only further strengthen our relationship with them and add to the growing list of benefits they provide us. Lucky us.

ACKNOWLEDGMENTS

I would like to acknowledge all of the dog lovers and seekers of knowledge who helped shape this book. Thanks to Alix Garcia, who wondered aloud about the anatomy of her puppy. Thanks to puppy Bella Garcia, for flopping over on her back so that Alix could rub her belly and pique her curiosity. And thanks to their mom, Karen Garcia, for picking up the phone and setting this project in motion!

I also gratefully acknowledge my panel of experts: Susan Helmink, Michael Berkenblit, and Lorraine Kassarjian, who tirelessly answered questions that only seemed to bring more questions, and patiently and repeatedly explained complicated concepts.

I appreciate the efforts of my agent, Lauren Abramo, who believed in the suggestion that ours is a nation of dog lovers, and Jennifer Kushnier, the editor who put up with my constant e-mails and queries with a good nature and positive, friendly attitude. Thank you both for making the process a pleasant one. To my project manager at Adams Media, Katrina Schroeder, thank you for your hard work and cooperative spirit. If I thought it would be appreciated, I would buy you all a big bone!

To the humane educators and especially the Association of Professional Humane Educators (APHE), a group composed of curious and tenacious animal lovers, thank you for being so supportive and for finding new ways to look at old theories. Thanks, especially, to Liz Baranowski of the Pasadena Humane Society for her assistance and friendship throughout this project. She's truly a walking "dog encyclopedia"!

I want to thank my parents, Kathleen and George Lake, who respected animals and taught me to always look at them in wonder and awe. I especially want to thank my sister, Kerry Lake, who instilled in me a passion for dogs when I was just a little girl. Her infectious knowledge and love of dogs was the basis for my own obsession.

And most of all, I thank my family: my husband, John; our sons, Toby and Jay, and their wives and children, who suffer my animal devotion with good nature and humor. I love you all.

INTRODUCTION

Alix Garcia loves to play rough-and-tumble with her Golden Retriever puppy, Bella. The girls engage in playful wrestling, their favorite activity. It was during one such play session on a sunny Florida afternoon that ten-year-old Alix turned Bella onto her back and rubbed her tummy, the way she had been taught, in order to signal that playtime was over and to help quiet Bella. As she did so, Alix considered the puppy's soft, fat pinkness under all that downy yellow fur and asked, "Mommy, does Bella have a belly button?" Karen Garcia looked at her daughter in amazement. Kids are so good at coming up with puzzling questions—and this was a doozy! Stumped, she answered, "That's a great question, and I have no idea what the answer is. They must, right?" Alix agreed, but that only brought up more questions: "Where is it? Why can't I see it like I can see my belly button? Don't all babies have belly buttons? Are they innies or outties? If they don't, then how do they get their food from their moms before birth?"

With an estimated 57 million animal lovers in the United States, someone, sometime, somewhere, is asking himself (or his mom, best friend, or even his cat) just this kind of question. These are the questions one would love to ask a good friend who just happens to be a vet. Since not everyone has a bosom buddy who went to veterinary school, we thought a friendly book that addresses this and other such questions was way overdue!

This is a book about our fascination with, and misunderstanding of, our best friend, the canine. Lovers of dogs observe them close up and afar, but close observation is likely to bring more questions, not answers.

I have been a humane educator for many years and have dedicated my life to learning about animals and their idiosyncrasies. I am fanatical in my curiosity about all things having to do with animals and I am constantly reading, learning, researching, and asking "Why?" when it comes to animal behavior. Not only will you benefit from that ardent curiosity (and discover your own inquisitiveness, as well), but so will your dog. Understanding and communication is, of course, the key to any great relationship. In my capacity as a humane educator, veterinary technician, and animal writer, I get to hang out with experts who will be helping us understand the answers to some burning questions. Our panel comprises two veterinarians, a few dog trainers, a professor of animal sciences, and humane educators from all over the country. All are well suited to entertain these universal mysteries. Let's gather around the fire and talk about our favorite subject: dogs!

You can say any fool thing to

a dog, and the dog will give you

this look that says, 'My God,

you're RIGHT! I NEVER would've

thought of that!'

—Dave Barry

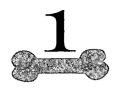

POOCH PARTS:
HOW A DOG'S BODY WORKS

Q. Do dogs have belly buttons?

A. Dogs are mammals. This means they bear their young alive (as opposed to laying an egg). A puppy developing in utero requires rich nutrients from his mother. Just as with a human baby, a prenatal puppy (or any mammal) receives that nutrition through the umbilical cord, a flexible tube that connects the growing puppy with the mother so she can provide him with food and nutrients until he is born. When a puppy is born, his mother chews through the cord, leaving a vestige of it that will eventually just fall off of the puppy, having lost its source of oxygen. This leaves a tiny scar. On people, this scar is called a belly button!

As baby animals grow, the soft, tender belly skin stretches until the navel scar is practically eliminated. This presents a big challenge for many animal shelter workers when admitting a female dog with no history, such as a stray. It is very difficult to tell if that scar is from a spay or if that tiny line is just the belly button. When a female animal is spayed, the scar replaces that tiny line.

Q. Are dogs related to wolves?

A. The DNA of a wolf and that of a dog is virtually the same, so dogs are most definitely related to wolves. Dogs and wolves compose a small percentage of the estimated thirty-eight species in the dog family, Canidae. The fully domesticated dog belongs to the subspecies *Canis familiaris.*

Wolves and dogs share many traits. They both rely on body language to communicate with one another. The respective positions of the hackles (the fur line that runs from the dog's neck to his tail, or along his spine), ears, tail, and mouth and the expression in his eyes are all important indicators upon which a wolf will rely to determine what state of mind a possible opponent or mate is in. Domestic dogs also use body language, but because selective breeding among dogs has produced breeds with drooping ears, docked tails, and long coats, the effectiveness of body language is arguable. If a dog holds his ears up and tight, or flattened against his head, he's communicating that he's alert to any danger. If he stares at you—unblinking and defiant—he's challenging you to a fight. If his tail is held tucked between his legs, he is letting you know he's afraid. It's much the same way with wolves.

Dogs have been with us since the ice age and were the first animal to be domesticated and befriended by humans, so it's no surprise that we have learned to read one another's body language. The relationship has been symbiotic ever since the beginning, when wolves first started hanging around the campfire.

FUR FACT

Some dogs, such as Newfoundlands and Standard Poodles, have webbed feet, just like a duck! That is the hallmark of a water dog (a dog that was bred to work in the water). Poodles were once used to retrieve fallen birds in the water, and Newfoundlands were bred to rescue swimmers in trouble.

Q. Do dogs really only see in black and white?

A. To completely understand how dogs view the world, we would have to ask one. But since we can't, we have to rely on science. There's a difference between the canine eye and the human eye, and the difference has to do with the parts of the eye called rods and cones. It is the cones that are responsible for allowing us to appreciate and perceive color. The rods are for distinguishing shapes and sizes, as well as black and white. What we do know is that a dog's eye has more rods than cones. Also, the canine eye has more rods than does the human eye. This has given rise to the theory that dogs see mostly in shades of gray, with very little color. Dogs can see better at dusk than we can, because their eyes are suited to detecting movement in the dark. Since wolves are nocturnal hunters and dogs are related to wolves, this makes sense.

If you look out your window just after the sun goes down, you will notice that your neighbor's bright red Corvette is duller at that time of day than it is when the sun is shining. This will give you a good idea of how dogs see the world all the time.

Q. Why do dogs gray heavier around their eyes and mouth when they age?

A. In order to answer this question we have to understand how color gets to the fur in the first place. Fur color is the result of pigment. Pigment is manufactured and stored in the hair follicles. As the fur grows, it grabs some of the pigment from the follicle and colors the strand. Just as with a human, as he ages, a dog's body makes less pigment, and there comes a time when there is very little or no pigment left. So, with the absence of pigment, the hair grows without color. Even though pigment is manufactured by your body, there is a finite amount. So when it runs out, that's it. We sometimes see the same thing with humans; for instance, a man may have jet-black hair but

FUR FACT

Can you kiss your dog on the lips? Nope, cause he ain't got lips! He's got flews!

his mustache or beard will be gray or streaked with gray. Scientists have not determined why there is less pigment on the face than elsewhere on the body.

Q. Why do dogs have whiskers?

A. Whiskers are found on many fur-bearing animals, including people, and even on a few species of bottom-feeding fish. They are most obvious on either side of the dog's snout, but whiskers also grow above his eyebrows, on his chin, and even on the upper lip, like a mustache.

Whiskers are coarse hairs that have a hardened, unique cellular composition. The purpose of the whiskers in mice and cats is to help these critters squeeze into small spaces, as they frequently do. The whiskers give the animal the information it needs to know if it can make it through the space.

However, experts don't think that whiskers on dogs provide the same information. Some experts believe that the purpose of the dog's whiskers is to help the dog comprehend his surroundings. They serve as delicate sense organs and help the dog pick up on vibrations carried on air currents. As the air moves around the whiskers, the dog processes information in the vibrations, much as whales and dolphins use echolocation. Whiskers also function as eye protectors, and when the whiskers are disturbed, the dog's eyes will sometimes close in anticipation of an irritant.

FUR FACT

There is a breed of dog that cannot bark. Commonly known as "The Barkless Dog," the Basenji, originating Africa, has a sort of "chortle" instead of a bark.

Like hair, whiskers also have roots, but the roots are three times deeper than the hair follicle, and are much stronger and sturdier than the average hair. This area, where the whiskers meet the skin and below, is extremely sensitive, so whiskers should never be pulled.

Despite all that's known about dogs' whiskers, groomers routinely shave them off of their clients' dogs for aesthetic reasons. The dogs don't seem to suffer from this indignity, so perhaps the whiskers have outgrown their original purposes. "To cut or not to cut" the whiskers off your dog is a big, important decision in his life, so be sure to get the advice of the canine fashion police. Today's "petrosexual" dog must, above all, be chic and well groomed!

Q. Why do different-size dogs have different-sounding barks?

A. This is definitely a case of "size does matter" because the voice of a dog, or his bark, comes from his larynx, just as your voice comes from your own larynx. The larynx is made of bones and connective tissue. The bones and ligaments line up to form a kind of boxy shape—that's where we get the term "voice box." If you gently feel your dog's throat, you can usually feel the larynx, if he'll let you. So the depth of the dog's bark is relative to the size of the dog's voice box. It's similar to the sound produced by bells. A big bell has a deeper and more resonant sound than a little bell, which sounds tinny by comparison. So the bigger the dog, the bigger the larynx, which produces a bigger, deeper bark.

There are anomalies, however, and sometimes you will find a big dog with a little wimpy bark. In that case, it's just pure genetics and anatomy. In other words, the big dog was shafted in the larynx department; a genetic problem produced a small voice box. Most of a dog's anatomy corresponds to his size—big dog, big paws; little dog, little paws—except in the case of a genetic problem that causes a mutation, which is not a common medical condition.

Q. Do dogs sweat?

A. The word for how our bodies regulate our core temperature is "thermoregulation." The body temperature of a human is normally 98.6°F, and a dog's is 101.5°F. While perspiration (sweat) is our principal means of keeping cool, a dog's core temperature is kept at an even level by panting. The act of panting causes increased air flow over moist surfaces (tongue and flews) and cools the respiratory tract, which in turn keeps the dog cool. Inhaled air proceeds to the lungs, where it is warmed and then exhaled, expelling the heat with it. Dogs do have sweat glands on their paws and in their ear canals, but those glands play a small part, if any, in keeping them cool. So the official answer is, no, dogs do not sweat as a method of thermoregulation.

Due to the way their bodies keep them cool, heat can be detrimental to dogs. A dog left in a hot car, for example, will quickly die because he cannot lower his body temperature. Circulation coming in over the tongue and nose will be full of hot air, a condition I call the "Politicians' syndrome," a situation that's never good for anyone. Dogs with short, pushed-in faces (called brachycephalic), such as Bulldogs and Pugs, are more susceptible to the heat by virtue of their very short noses. The air does not have the time to cool before it enters the body. Also, dogs with long hair or dark fur heat up much faster than do lighter-colored, short-haired dogs, so their exposure to direct sunlight and hot days should be limited.

Q. What are dewclaws, and why do dogs have them?

A. First, we need to identify what the deal is with the dews. A dewclaw is a superfluous toe/claw that is located on the back of the hock (ankle) of a dog's legs. Dewclaws are usually seen on the rear legs. The claw does not reach the ground and just dangles there looking very undignified and silly. The dewclaws are sometimes connected to the bone, as are the other digits, or can simply be connected to the skin, which makes them floppy and presents a danger to dogs who spend a lot of time in the woods. A dog used for hunting is especially prone to injury because the dewclaws can get snagged by thorny branches, causing lacerations. Dewclaws are vascular and bleed prolifically when torn.

Veterinarians are not sure why modern dogs have dewclaws or what their original function may have been in wild animals. It is generally accepted that the front ones are a holdover from the evolutionary process, and at some point they may have been used almost as a thumb. However, most veterinarians agree that dewclaws should be removed because of the potential for cuts and scrapes, which could lead to infection. Dewclaws are best removed when the dog is still a puppy, as the experience

> **FUR FACT**
>
> Dogs that are sterilized at an early age, around six to nine months, are less likely to develop cancer in later years. Dogs not sterilized (intact) have a much higher risk of developing testicular, ovarian, prostate, mammary, and uterine cancer by the time they are six years old.

is less stressful at that age. Ideally, this is done during a spay/neuter surgery.

Q. Why do dogs drool?

A. Some dogs do seem to be a little "juicier" than others, don't they? Who can forget the scene in *Beethoven* where the big lovable Saint Bernard, having been caught napping on the bed, showers Charles Grodin with lots of goopy goo. Ahh, ya gotta love 'em! The beloved Saint Bernard is just one of many breeds that tend to drool much more than do their drier cousins. The Bassett Hound, Bullmastiff, Irish Water Spaniel, and Bloodhounds are among canines' top droolers. These dogs are not actually making more saliva (slobber) than other dogs, it's just that the flews, or lips, are droopier and the skin around them saggier. This allows for the saliva to drip out instead of being neatly contained within the dog's mouth. Dogs drool for the same reason that a baby, or a person asleep with his mouth open, does: no watertight seal!

If your normally non-drooling dog suddenly becomes a drooler, however, it's time for a trip to the vet. There could be a dental or gum problem, or even a toxic substance in your dog's mouth that requires the skills of a veterinarian. Or it could simply be a piece of twig or other irritant that you can remove yourself. Then again, it might just be good old Pavlov's theory of conditioning. In the early 1900s, Russian scientist Ivan Pavlov found that he could condition his dogs to salivate upon hearing the sound of a bell, which promised food. So some dogs, when offered food, will salivate excessively in anticipation of the taste of that food.

Q. Why do dogs get those ugly bumpy things on their elbows?

A. Dogs get calluses on their elbows from lying on the floor. It used to be thought that only dogs who lie on concrete all day get these spots, but there is many a pampered pet out there living in the lap of luxury and sporting ugly elbow calluses. In many cases, when a dog lies down, the elbows are the first thing to hit the ground. Whether dogs are lying on their bellies or on their sides, their front legs are usually resting on the floor on their elbows, which makes them pressure points. All this rubbing and contact with carpeting, tile, or cement serves to roughen and toughen the dog's elbows. Like the hardening and roughing-up of our heels when we go barefoot all the time, a dog's elbows bear the brunt of day-to-day life. Naturally, the calluses worsen with time, so they're considered a symptom of old age. They may not be aesthetically pleasing, but they're harmless and don't hurt the dog. Big dogs are more prone to calluses because they are putting more weight on the elbows than are little dogs, thereby adding more stress.

Q. Why do dogs' tongues hang out?

A. When a dog is relaxed and feeling camaraderie with those around him, he relaxes his mouth in sort of a doggy smile. His eyes take on a soft countenance and his lips may draw back slightly. This is pure doggy friendship, the canine version of when we kick back with our friends, bantering and enjoying a pleasant time together. A dog's tongue hanging loosely when he is in this state is a natural occurrence because his mouth and jaw muscles, including the muscles that hold the tongue, are not tensed.

However, in some cases, it could also be a symptom of a problem. If a dog's tongue is hanging out, appears bright red, and there is

> **FUR FACT**
> A female dog is correctly called a "bitch" and a mother dog is called a "dam." A dog that fathers a litter is called a "sire."

FUR FACT

If you are worried about doggy odor and want to keep your dog from excessive shedding or odor, don't over-bathe him. Excessive bathing only dries out the skin, which actually causes more dander to be released into the air. Natural oils in the dog's skin and coat help keep the dander down and the coat nice and shiny. And when bathing your dog, be sure to use a nondrying, conditioning shampoo made just for dogs.

excessive salivation, it could signify heat stroke or another shock-inducing situation. Because dogs regulate their body temperature differently than we do (by panting) their tongues may hang limply out of their mouths naturally as a way of heat control.

Q. Why do dogs shed?

A. Shedding is a natural thing in the animal kingdom, *Homo sapiens* included. Just as we lose hair to accommodate new growth and snakes shed their skin to accommodate new skin, dogs shed to allow new growth to come in and to ready themselves for the coming warmer months. A dog will "blow his coat," as it is called in the dog world, when the summer is approaching and he no longer needs a thick, insulating layer of fur. Today's modern dogs generally live indoors in a temperature-controlled atmosphere, causing them not to experience a drastic seasonal change. Because of this, they may shed all year round.

Some dogs have fur that is more like hair, and they don't shed much at all. These dogs are sometimes listed as "hypoallergenic dogs." On the other hand, some, such as Siberian Huskies or Newfoundlands, have thick undercoats in addition to their regular coats, and those dogs tend to shed much more. Then there are dogs with no coat at all, such as the Chinese Crested or the Mexican Hairless. They must wear sweaters and coats to keep warm in cooler climates.

In order to really enjoy a dog,

one doesn't merely try to train

him to be semi-human. The point

of it is to open oneself to the

possibility of becoming partly

a dog.

—Edward Hoagland

DOGGY DEEDS: WHY DOGS DO THE THINGS THEY DO

Q. Why do dogs eat a good pair of slippers?

A. This is an easy one. Dogs love the smell of things that we humans think smell really bad. We see dogs rolling in dead things and carrying around some funky stuffed toy that has slobber on it dating back to the administration of the first President Bush! So what we perceive as stinky foot smell is more like Slipper Sweat Sweet Treat to dogs! Dogs also adore anything that smells like their human. Your slippers have taken on a fragrance of their own and because of that, they call to your pooch, who will happily settle in for a nice, long chew. Experts say that it's never a good idea to give your dog an old, discarded slipper to chew on because dogs cannot distinguish between the old discarded one that he can have, and the brand-new faux fur sequin-studded slippers he cannot have.

Dogs are also great opportunists. They will take advantage of any opportunity to find things on which to gnaw, or even eat, without regard to the fact that the charge for those bunny slippers hasn't even shown up on your credit card yet! Since we tend to leave slippers lying about the floor rather than up high on a shoe rack, dogs can get to them quite easily. And if you do, in fact, have bunny slippers (or gorilla slippers for you manly men), they look a lot like the stuffed toys we buy at the pet store, so it's easy to see how confusing the whole affair can be to your pooch.

Lonely dogs will also chew to pass the time and as a way to bond with the human who has left his delectable sweaty scent on the slippers. The act of chewing seems to have sedative properties, helping keep the dog calm and composed. Just remember, no matter how many slippers or Nike sneakers or Prada slingbacks he chews, he really does love you!

Q. Why do dogs yawn?

A. Dogs yawn out of boredom, anxiety, confusion, and sometimes because they are tired. If you want to make your dog yawn, do your impression of Tina Turner singing "Proud Mary" or Elvis, the early years. This makes a dog yawn because he doesn't understand what your body language is trying to tell him and he is confused. Body language is one of the most effective ways for dogs to communicate with us and with each other. Since your dog can't understand the gyrating, the arm swinging, the twirling, and the high-pitched musical styling showcased in your lyrical performances, he gets confused. Yawning is what is called a "displacement signal." Also called "calming signals," these are signs that dogs exhibit during times of stress. They do seem to help calm the dog. Other calming signals include lip licking and avoidance of eye contact.

Much like we do with yoga breathing or stretching, calming signals help the dog cope with whatever it is that is causing the stress. Yawning brings oxygen quickly to the lungs. We yawn when we are tired or bored because our body is trying to wake us up, make us more alert. Dogs also yawn to bring oxygen to the lungs to make ready for fight or flight, if they are stressed out. For example, a dog who is sitting in an unattended car and is approached by a stranger may feel angry and protective, or he may feel threatened. If he does, in fact, feel threatened, he may yawn, break eye contact, lick his lips, or suddenly become absorbed in the fabric pattern on the seat in an effort to distract himself. So if your dog is yawning, don't automatically assume it's nap time. It may be time for a nap, but most likely, there's something that's bothering him.

Q. Why does a dog sniff the ground?

A. Humor writer Dave Barry once said: "Dogs need to sniff the ground; it's how they keep abreast of current events. The ground is a giant dog newspaper, containing all kinds of late-breaking news items, which, if they are especially urgent, are often continued in the next yard."

Just as we read the paper to find out what is happening in the world around us, dogs sniff the ground to check out what's happening in the neighborhood. All the dogs who have ever walked that mile; all the urine that has ever been dribbled, sprayed, or streamed; all the feces; all the fur and the fleas that have ever dropped off a dog, or cat, or other animal (people included)—all of this leaves residue on the ground that the dog, with his undeniably fabulous sense of smell, can pick up and use in ways we cannot imagine. We want peace in the world. Dogs want pees in the world! They can tell if there is a turf war going on in their neighborhood or park. They know who all the usual suspects are, and they know when a new dog has hit the scene. They can tell if the new dog is a huge, male alpha dog, a force to be reckoned with, or a puppy with pink bows. Okay, maybe they don't know if she's got bows, but they can tell an awful lot about the animals on their street. Mr. Rogers sang about the importance of getting to know the people in your neighborhood. Your dog is just trying to determine who the doggies in his neighborhood are, if they are well or ill, if they are in heat, if they have recently eaten something delectable (because possibly there's more where that came from!). Dogs are opportunistic in every way. Taking opportunities to learn about the animals who share his world is a dog's greatest joy. And, the mystery of how dogs find their way home after taking themselves for a walk outside the fence is solved. Like bread crumbs, urine spots lead the way.

Q. Is it bad to smile at a strange dog?

A. Let's think about the ways that dogs communicate with us. They wag their tails, they roll over on their backs, and, oh joy, they even deign to pee on us. One of the most dramatic and no-nonsense things dogs do is bare their teeth. When a dog shows his teeth, he has moved past the barking warnings and is swiftly moving toward the biting part because when he shows his teeth, he is actually demonstrating aggression. So if you look at it from the dog's point of view, you can understand why dogs easily get confused when a stranger smiles at them. A dog who is familiar with you will not take the smile as a threat because that dog has learned to translate your entire body language very well. He is taking in your posture, the sounds you are making, your entire attitude, not just the showing of the teeth. When we smile, we show our teeth, but the smile usually reaches our eyes, which become merry with delight. A strange dog does not have a history with you; he has not learned to read your body language. So, smiling at a strange dog, especially one who may be fearful or angry, is probably not a good idea.

Q. Why do dogs "mouth" people?

A. Mouthing is the term for when a dog places his mouth gently on a part of your body, usually your arm, and holds it there. It is almost like biting except he does not bear down and leaves no marks. The pressure a dog uses while mouthing would be similar to that used to pick up her young. There are as many reasons why dogs do some of the things they do as there are dogs! A lot of the time, the reasoning behind mouthing depends on what else they are doing at the time. If they are playing, it could be an element of play. They don't have hands to play with things, so they use their mouths like we use our hands. Just as we may play with an object by juggling it or moving it around (stop playing with your food and read the book!), dogs use their mouths to do the same thing. In addition, dogs play with one another by mouthing, so they just carry over that behavior to their interactions with humans.

However, there may also be some latent Freudian reasons. Oh here we go, let's blame Mom! It could have something to do with having an oral fixation because it reminds them of happier times, when they were nursing and with their moms and siblings. It could also be a dominance thing. Dogs may mouth to get control of someone, to get the upper hand, so to speak, or maybe to direct the person. Mouthing is also something dogs do to calm themselves when they are

FUR FACT

Researchers are now using "scat dogs" to find the scat, or feces, of endangered or rare animals. Scientists have discovered that they can train dogs to locate rare-breed scat much faster than they themselves can do it.

bored, stressed, or nervous; it's a displacement signal, like when we bite our nails.

Professor and lecturer on animal sciences Susan Helmink adds, "It is simple normal exploratory behavior. Dogs—especially puppies—will mouth to explore their surroundings. They can't pick things up and feel them with their paws, so their mouths are their guide. Dogs mouth each other in play, as well. Mouthing could also be construed as a 'hug' of sorts. I know quite a few dogs who take a hold of a person's arm in greeting, especially if it is someone they know well. I have observed this mostly in retriever-type dogs—who like to put things in their mouths—but I also know working dogs that do it, perhaps because of the strong bond they have for their human pack."

Q. Why do dogs turn in circles before lying down?

A. In the wild, there are tree dwellers, land dwellers, and earth dwellers. Tree dwellers, such as many species of monkeys and marsupials, will sleep in trees. Earth dwellers, such as moles, prairie dogs, and meerkats, live underground, under the earth. Land dwellers, such as the big cats and wolves, live and sleep on the land, so they are required to make appropriate sleeping arrangements. Animals that forage for their food, or that hunt down prey, often follow that prey for long distances and so are required to make a new bed for themselves every night. Since they can't very well access Hotels.com, they are forced to provide their own sleeping quarters. This is how the circling came to be. In the wild, wolves find a place with very tall grasses that will shield them from other predators while they sleep. In order to make a comfortable bed for themselves, they circle and circle and circle a spot, tamping down the tall grasses into a nice, cushy mattress for themselves.

Snow dogs do this too, packing the snow to make a bed. Their body heat causes the snow to melt a little and a cradle of ice forms. The dog lies down; the snow covers him, and keeps him warm. Ice is a good insulator; it will maintain the heat coming from the dog's body.

Doing things like this is what's known as "throwback behavior," meaning it's a throwback to the days of wolves in the wild. Even though you have purchased the best doggy bed money can buy, your dog will still circle once or twice out of a sense of habit or ingrained instinct, a nod to his wild ancestors.

Q. Why do dogs wag their tails?

A. We love to see dogs who are full-fledged, card-carrying members of the Tailwaggers' Coalition! Wagging their tails means they are happy, right? Well, maybe. The motion actually had a function in the wild. The anal glands, located just inside the anus, emit a scent that, thankfully, we humans cannot smell, but other dogs do. The wagging tail is intended to spread the scent around, sort of like when we spray the house with room freshener. When dogs are happy, they want others to know they are there and ready to party! But there are times when a wagging tail can signal danger; a motion doggy folks call "flagging." It's dog-speak for "don't come near, I'm afraid." When a dog is wagging his tail slowly from side to side and the tail is stiff, coupled with showing the teeth and raising the hackles, it's not a friendly wagging, it's a danger sign. Tail carriage (the position in which a dog carries his tail) can give us lots of clues as to what a dog may be thinking. A dog's tail can communicate all kinds of things, such as heightened awareness or interest, fear,

FUR FACT

Which dog is mentioned in the Bible? The word "dog" is mentioned forty times in the Bible, but only one breed is mentioned by name, and that is the Greyhound. (Proverbs 30:31)

defiance, confusion, or aggression. Watch your dog when he's watching a squirrel, and you'll see the tail take on a full vertical, very still position. But if he's looking for a fight or to challenge an opponent (real or imagined), his tail may be horizontal and held fast. A dog with his tail between his legs is a submissive, fearful dog.

Q. Why do dogs roll in dead things?

A. To a dog, a dead, rotting animal on the ground smells a lot like Chanel N° 5 does to those of us who love it. This inexplicable habit of rolling around in something horrid is one of those things that dogs do that make us wonder if we really should be letting them spoon under the covers with us. There are various theories as to why modern dogs do this. Some think it is a throwback to their wolf days, when they would roll around in carcasses or feces to mask their own scent so that they could sneak up on prey. It's not all that far-fetched to think your Chihuahua is acting out wolf tendencies.

This need to roll around in smelly things happens particularly after a dog has had a bath. The reason for this is that many dog-bath products are perfumed to please human consumers. But dogs find it unpleasant to carry such a strong odor, especially one they find annoying and ridiculous. In an effort to cover up that scent, they will roll around in the grass or anything else smelly and available, hoping to lose their scent and pick up another (and in *their* opinion a more suitable) doggy smell.

So what can you do about it? If this happens on a regular basis, you might try using an unscented dog shampoo; there is no roadkill-scented soap on the market just yet, thank goodness. Otherwise, keep your dog close to home and don't give him the opportunity to roll in smelly stuff . . . especially since he'll want to share your bed. And unless he snores (as if *you* don't), do let him sleep close to you. Dogs are pack animals; you're the pack. That's just the way it is.

Q. Can a neutered dog still get an erection?

A. When we neuter a dog, we take away his ability to make testosterone. But he still has the ability to get an erection. Penile erection is not necessarily related to testosterone; it's related to blood flowing to a dog's penis. Neutered dogs won't get an erection as often because their testosterone level is lowered and that, in turn, lowers their sexual interest. They can however, still have blood rushing to the area, but sometimes it has less to do with sex and more to do with joy.

Q. Why do some dogs urinate when they get excited?

A. This conduct is known to those who work with pets as "submissive urination." The dog will often crouch as low to the ground as he can in a display of submission, and then urinate. Dr. Lorraine Kassarjian believes that when it's only a couple of drops, the cause is very simple. "It may be because there is just a little urine left in the urethra, and when a dog becomes excited, all his muscles are tightening up, and whatever is in the urethra gets squeezed out from the muscle tension. Some dogs, however, will turn over on their backs and pee up in the air, a long stream, perhaps even targeting an individual."

Wolves in the wild submit this way to the alpha wolf, making it a throwback behavior dogs exhibit to show submission. Urine is what dogs use as a calling card, to leave their mark on people, places, and things. Dr. Lorraine (who goes by her first name due to the difficult pronunciation of her last name) says, "Perhaps turning over and peeing into the air is to mark the person or dog they are submitting to in order to say 'Hey, we smell the same, we are the same, I am part of your pack.'"

Q. Is it bad to look a dog directly in the eye?

A. Staring a dog directly in the eye is the doggy version of "You wanna step outside?" When you look a dog directly in the eye, you are challenging him to a fight. This is how dogs will pick a fight with other dogs, and this is how dogs will interpret it if you do it to them. It's very bad to look a dog directly in the eye or to allow your dog to stare down another household pet, a child, or a strange dog. When you see a dog glaring directly at someone or something, be ready to take action because your dog is picking a fight. It's a no-nonsense way of getting his point across: "I don't like you and here's what I am going to do about it!" Don't worry about confusing this with curious observation; you will know it when you see it because it's a very intentional and deliberate motion. You can't misinterpret this, as a dog's whole body will be telling you to be on guard.

Anyone who has been on the receiving end of this direct stare, especially if the dog is one of the big breeds such as a Rottweiler, Doberman Pinscher, or German

Shepherd Dog, knows the look. It can be very intimidating. A dog whose ear carriage is naturally tall and erect makes for a particularly formidable adversary. If you do see a dog looking at you like this, don't try a nervous little "nice doggy" while attempting to let him sniff you. The best strategy, experts say, is to look off to the side, so that the dog is still within your vision, but you are not looking directly at him, and stand very still. Eventually, the dog will become bored with you since you are just standing there, not creating a threat or doing anything interesting, and will move along on his own.

Q. Do dogs consider humans their "pack"?

A. Anyone who shares his space with a dog or two is fully aware that dogs are social animals. Virtually everyone who has a dog reports that their dog follows them around and hangs out wherever the human is hanging out. Indeed, some dogs have been known to sit by the bathroom door and whine because they just can't stand it when their human is out of sight.

Dogs also love to be with other dogs. But in the absence of other canines, will a human being suffice? Many experts believe that dogs are not that far removed from the wolf pack. Wolves are not lone animals; their very survival depends an awful lot on getting along with the rest of the group. They hunt together, they raise their young together, and together they protect their dens and territories. Nobody understands this better than Tammy Grimes, the founder of Dogs Deserve Better, a dog advocacy group whose mission is to stop people from chaining their dogs in the yard.

"Five years ago, before Dogs Deserve Better and even with my limited knowledge of dogs and packs, I would have answered 'probably' to this question [of whether humans can suffice as the pack]. But today, after five years of fostering formerly chained and penned dogs, I have to say an unqualified, most emphatic—YES!" says Tammy. "When I first remove the chains, dogs are often initially shy, frantic for attention, or even fearful, which may manifest itself as aggression. This is all due to a lack of socialization and quality human companionship. After little more than a day or two, they begin to integrate with the pack, finding their spot, and it's not long before they recognize me as pack leader. I know this because they 'hang out' wherever I am. In my home, which doubles as the Dogs Deserve Better headquarters and foster training center, we have two fenced areas and two doggy doors. In essence, these dogs could be outside all day long if they please, but they rarely are . . .

unless I am. They spend much of the day following me around the house, trying to get me to play with them or interact with them in some way. A lot like my own children!"

Tammy believes that a dog's social neediness is why chaining or penning him for life is truly the worst punishment man can mete out to dogs. As pack animals, they long to be with their family, their pack. Since the pack society of long ago no longer exists, we humans have in essence become their pack, and they suffer terribly when ostracized from us. They've been "thrown out" of the pack, and they don't know why. They stand looking toward the house, hoping against hope that their human pack members will come out and spend time with them; they act up, barking, whining, digging; or they give up and lie lethargically, not even bothering to show any excitement when a human comes outside.

FUR FACT

You may not be able to tell from looking at them, but no two Dalmatians have the same spot pattern. Just like every snowflake, these "firehouse" dogs are all unique.

As pack leaders, humans have to accept responsibility for the dogs who depend on us for their very survival. It's our job to ensure we are firm but loving with our dogs, so they can feel secure in their place in the pack, and we can have harmony in our households. In the wolf pack, a wolf that is kept away from the pack for some transgression panics because his chances of survival in the wild without his family are slim. A lone wolf cannot survive as well as a wolf pack, so it's no wonder a Beagle or Cocker Spaniel who is tied to a tree acts up; he thinks he's doomed.

Q. Is there such a thing as "top dog" in a pack?

A. It depends on the situation. In the wild, dogs clearly have a pack. The PBS video documentary *In the Company of Wolves* follows the trail of actor/activist/wolf researcher Timothy Dalton, who spent years traveling in search of wolf packs all over America and Canada and camping out with them. Dalton explains that wolves absolutely have a hierarchy system in which there is an alpha, or top, wolf and a lesser wolf, the omega wolf. Almost always, there's an alpha pair, which would be male/female. The alpha wolf or pair gets to eat first, seems to be the leader of the pack, and even takes out frustration and anger on the omega.

Some experts believe that there is a code among dogs that allows them to figure out who the top dog is. Dogs will test other dogs in a variety of ways. For example, let's say Fluffy and Pluto's owners have decided to bring these two dogs together for a play date. The dogs have heretofore not met, and they are about the same height and weight, maybe even the same breed. For the sake of our example, let's say Fluffy is a female and Pluto a male (although the same behavior could occur with two males or two females). After the initial meeting, Fluffy will want to show that she is the alpha dog. She may stand on her back feet and place her paws on Pluto's back. If Pluto allows that, Fluffy will attempt to stand over Pluto, by actually straddling Pluto. If Pluto allows that, Fluffy may even begin humping Pluto in an effort to show that she is the dominant of the two. If he simply adopts a "what the heck" attitude and allows her to do those things, Fluffy is the clear leader. However, if Pluto does not agree to let Fluffy be "in charge," then he won't allow her to stand on him, or over him, or hump him. He may even try to do those things to her instead, if he wants to challenge her for "top dog" position. If he challenges her, the testing will continue until one dog decides to submit. This is usually done by rolling over on one's back, exposing the belly. One of the dogs may also exhibit submission by licking the other dog's mouth. In any event, a leader is chosen.

Susan Helmink, a humane educator and lecturer on animal sciences, agrees, and wants dog owners to understand that "in a dog family, it's important to support whatever hierarchy is established between two dogs. However, some trainers caution against letting the dogs work it out for themselves because it can get out of hand. A submissive posture should turn off the dominant behaviors of the other dog, but unfortunately sometimes it does not. Similarly, in rare circumstances, I have heard of younger dogs bullying much older dogs when they can sense the dog is failing."

However, in most normal canine relationships, the younger, healthier dog won't even begin to contend, because there is no glory in winning a competition with a dog who is obviously so inferior. Out of deference or respect or just sheer understanding, the dogs seem to know that the dance is not necessary in this situation. In most cases with family dogs, it is the human who is accorded the role of "top dog" because it is the human who is the hunter/gatherer. (Unlike wolves, dogs accept humans as pack members.) The Pulitzer Prize–winning novelist Anne Tyler said, "Ever consider what our dogs must think of us? I mean, here we come back from the grocery store with . . . chicken, pork, half a cow! They must think we're the greatest hunters on Earth!"

And that's what makes us the top dog in the pack.

Q. Why do dogs fetch?

A. Fetching is, as so many other doggy deeds are, a throwback behavior. As predators, dogs are always on the lookout for prey. Prey moves. So motion of any kind will put your dog into motion as well. Something is moving, and he's on the case! During the early days of domestication, one of the very first things a dog did to earn his rightful place among humans was to teach us how to hunt. Cavemen didn't stand around the campfire alongside wolves singing "Kumbaya," but they did take note and were impressed by the prowess of the wolves, which worked together as a team to bring down their prey. In essence, they "fetched" it and brought it back to their pack. Over time, fetching was then used when people hunted with guns and arrows, and the prey would fall to the ground a considerable distance from the hunter. The dogs would go and fetch the prey and return it to the hunter.

Like the cat who brings lizards and mice home and leaves them for you in your bed, your dog is exhibiting behavior that says "I love you and I really want you to have this thing" when he brings back items you toss away.

Q. Why do male dogs lift their hind leg to pee? Why don't female dogs do it too?

A. You have e-mail, they've got pee mail! Remember the scene in *A Beautiful Mind* where the secret messages were only visible to Russell Crowe/John Nash? Dogs leave their scent behind for other dogs; when they tinkle on a vertical object, such as a fire hydrant, a tree, a fence, or your leg, they are sending a message that they have passed by and may still be in the area. The next dog that comes along will sniff the area, determine that another dog has been around fairly recently, and will lift his own leg to cover the scent of the first dog. It's a sort of DoggyMatch.com. A female dog will leave her scent, saying "Young, blond, hip, non-sterile female who eats chicken and veggies looking for dark and handsome intact male for a spring fling." The male dog will come along and answer the ad: "Grover here, I'm a young stud who eats burgers and fries and I'm ready for love," but then a third dog comes along and, using his urine, will say "Hey Grover! Move over because I'm the big shot in these parts." He says that by aiming his pee in such a way that it goes higher on the tree than Grover's did but also covers up Grover's scent!

A male puppy begins to lift his leg at about the age of six months. Usually, when the dog's owner sees him do this for the first time, it marks a rite of passage. Dogs don't have confirmation or bar mitzvah, so they do this instead! It shows they are on their way to adulthood.

Male dogs are more interested in finding a mate than female dogs are, and much more in tune with their competition in the wild (your street). Raising the leg allows the urine to stream upward and land in a spot just about where the next dog's nose will be. They try to make their stream go even higher in an effort to give the impression to other dogs that they are bigger than they are. Even neutered dogs will get into the act because it is more an exercise in social order than an actual dating service. You won't see the scent marking as much in doggy day-care centers or dog parks because the dogs are already there and on common ground, so there's not a lot of posturing going on.

Female dogs don't have the need to be so aggressive in their marketing, which is why they don't pee with one leg raised. It's usually the male of the species that comes calling, not the other way around. Owners of male dogs, especially nonsterilized ones, report that when they go for walks the dog seems to have a dribble or drop for every blade of grass, making it frustrating for those who want to get out, get in, and get it over with already!

Q. Can dogs be trained to use a litter box?

A. There are many products on the market that are offered to respond to the needs of dogs living in high-rise condos, aboard seagoing vessels, or living with shut-ins. There are litter boxes, similar to the kind a pussycat uses, but larger, as well as puppy pads, and even huge trays that hold sod or grasslike materials. Unlike cats, however, dogs would need to be trained to use the equipment because they do not naturally bury their feces like cats do. Most dogs catch on pretty quickly and will use the doggie box once they understand that it's their place. There are products on the market that contain artificial pheromones that will attract the dog to the area as well. Teaching dogs to use an indoor potty is a great convenience to those who have a service dog and would like to go on a cruise, people who have trouble walking their dog, or those living in cities that might be dangerous places for walking dogs, especially at night.

Q. Why don't dogs bury their feces like cats do?

A. Felines bury their waste because cats are covert creatures. They don't like to advertise their whereabouts, and prefer to avoid trouble rather than confront it. However, there are some cats who are possessed of more dominant personalities. Those cats will actually leave their feces out so that other cats will see it and recognize that there is a bigger, badder cat in the neighborhood, so everyone just better watch out! Dogs, unlike cats, have no secrets. They leave messages for one another in their excrement and hope that it will bring them lots of friends and lovers. Mostly lovers.

Q. Why do some dogs eat sometimes harmful, non-food items?

A. Often, the non-food item the dog is eating is feces. The medical term for doing this is "coprophagia" (coprow-FAIJ-ee-ah). Despite the fact that it totally disgusts us, it's somewhat normal for dogs to do this. Nursing mother dogs do it all the time to keep their dens clean and to hide the fact that there are vulnerable puppies in the vicinity. Some veterinarians believe that dogs will engage in coprophagia because they suffer from a nutritional deficiency. Dogs not only eat the feces of their puppies, but will snack on the leavings of other animals such as cats and rabbits as well. Some pet dogs who cohabit with cats will steal a few morsels from the litter box . . . completely unnerving their owners as they stare in shock at their cute little "Muffin Cake," who has potty mouth (literally) and kitty litter sprinkled about her carefully groomed snout! This problem is so common that there are products on the market you can feed to your cat to make his excrement taste bad so your dog won't seek it out.

The condition of eating other non-food items is called "pica" (pike-a). With puppies, it involves teething and chewing. Because puppies are breaking in adult teeth, they will chew just about anything they can get their paws on. Sometimes, these things are then swallowed. You won't believe some of the things vets have pulled from the innards of puppies. I once assisted in the removal of an entire, undamaged underwire bra from a puppy's intestines. The puppy's owner, a woman whose tiny breast size probably saved her dog's life, had a reason to be grateful she had put off that breast augmentation surgery!

There are also reasons for pica related to dietary needs. Dr. Lorraine relates a story of a patient of hers that could not seem to get enough rust. He would lick anything that was rusty, as if he were addicted to it. "I think there may have been some iron-deficiency issues there," she laughs. "There was something lacking in his diet and his body knew it, and he was trying to compensate for that deficiency."

And in case you're wondering (as I was), his name wasn't Rusty.

Q. Why do dogs howl?

A. Dogs have found a variety of ways to communicate with us and one another. While body language is certainly by far the most efficient way for dogs to communicate with each other and with savvy humans, vocal language is just as important. There are five main classes of vocal communication devices that dogs and wolves use to communicate over long distances: howling, barking, grunting, whining, and growling. When dogs howl they do so because they feel that barking alone will not reach the distances needed to get their message out. Pet owners who leave their dogs home alone for hours at a time will hear neighbors report (complain) that their dog has been howling. Think of it as a long-distance call from your dog! Often dogs will howl at the sound of a siren or in accompaniment to someone singing nearby. Some researchers believe they are simply joining in with the singing, and answering the call of the siren. Others believe that the sound is hurting their ears, so they are howling to make it stop. It could very well be simply the emotional pain of separation from the one he loves that causes the howling. Once again, we look to the wolves to explain dog behavior. Wolves howl to announce their availability for mating, warn other wolves of their territory, and communicate with their own pack. Most likely, dogs howl for many of the same reasons.

Q. Why do dogs chase squirrels, bunnies, and birds?

A. A lot of dogs, though domesticated, still have a strong prey drive, which is activated by motion of any kind. Since moving prey meant a possible snack for hungry wolves, today's dogs still can't help giving chase when they see something moving: That idea of "goal" is still ingrained in them. It's just the nature of the beast.

Another reason dogs will chase squirrels is out of a sense of protecting their territory. They see the backyard as an extension of their homes. A squirrel, or any other unfortunate little furry or feathery thing that happens into the yard, will be soundly rebuked and chased off the property. Your dog will then look to you for the appreciation and abject admiration he just knows will be there.

This is why laws exist to ensure that all domesticated animals are vaccinated against rabies. Depending on where you live, the chances that your dog may tussle with a rabies-vector species when you let him out to pee at 11:00 at night are relatively high. Of course, any squirrel with any pride at all can easily outrun a dog and escape by running up a tree.

I used this knowledge of prey drive when I first introduced a Siamese kitten into my household. The other two resident cats had long ago learned to stand firm when our dog Tyrone looked their way. But Maggie the Meezer (a "Siameezer") hadn't gotten the memo, and the two older cats weren't giving anything away. So Tyrone took to chasing Maggie the Meezer whenever she ran, making for quite a hectic home life. But instead of trying to teach an old dog a new trick, I trained little Maggie the Meezer to stand her ground. I held her close and petted her in front of Tyrone, making sure he understood that her position in the hierarchy was very high and she was a protected member of the pack. In this way, he learned to leave her alone or he'd answer to me, the "alpha bitch" in charge.

Q. Are Dalmatians born with their spots?

A. According to Joanne Nash, education chairperson of the Dalmatian Club of America, Dalmatians puppies are born pure white. "When they are very new and are still wet," explains Joanne, "signs of spotting on the skin may be visible—giving a hint of whether that pup will be heavily marked or have more open markings. Once dry, the hair is clean and white, and the skin spotting isn't evident. Hair is very short on the ears and face at this stage, and some spotting on the skin can be seen through this. Wherever there is skin spotting, the new coat will come in with pigmented hair. Spotting on the skin is more easily seen in black-spotted pups than in livers (brown-spotted). Breeders can usually tell at birth whether a puppy is black or liver by looking at the pigment on his nose and/or eye rims."

Q. Could a domesticated family dog ever live in the wild?

A. It is doubtful that a domesticated family dog could survive in the wild after living in a home. Dogs attach great meaning to people, places, and things, and become very despondent and desperate when they have been abandoned. Domesticated dogs are not knowledgeable about things that can harm them, such as cars, wild animals, and cruel people. They are not adept at finding food and will quickly succumb to the health problems created by exposure to excessive heat or cold, internal and external parasites such as worms and ticks, and injuries inflicted by cars, kids with BB guns, and tussles with wild animals.

If forced to live in the wild, a dog may make a valiant but mostly vain effort to survive. Most dogs will seek out a pack in which to ingratiate themselves, believing that living in a pack will give them a higher chance of successful living in the wild. But that brings with it its own dangers because those already in the pack will be slow to accept a newcomer, and the resources such as food and water will be strained when shared among all the members of the pack.

Many dogs have become skillful at dodging cars and running from people, locations, and objects when their instincts warn them of possible danger, but that learning process takes time, and time is usually not on the side of the dog. Luckily, most states have adopted laws against abandoning an animal that has been living a domesticated life because doing so is considered animal cruelty. After Hurricane Katrina, the dogs who survived the initial flooding were found wandering in packs and trying to survive. However, the tainted water, lack of food, and extreme summer heat all worked against them, and many succumbed to the elements.

Q. Why do dogs feel threatened by and try to chase the letter carrier?

A. Dogs have an amazing sense of territory and place a high priority on keeping families together and protecting loved ones. Dogs chase the letter carrier, the meter reader, the UPS guy, and anyone else with whom they are not familiar because they see that person as an intruder that needs to be stopped in his tracks. Any person who dares to come close to the dog's "den" (your house) and tread on his territory (your yard) is perceived as a potential threat. But why, specifically, do they go after letter carriers? Look at this from the dog's point of view. Same guy comes to the door every day, dog chases him or barks, guy leaves. The chasing or barking must be working, so he continues the behavior. A life-skills coach may say "How's that workin' for ya?" For the dog, it's working fine! To stop this behavior, try giving the letter carrier a few tasty tidbits with which to bribe your dog. Turns a foe into a friend!

Q. Why do dogs chase their tails?

A. Ah, that's a funny sight, isn't it? Dogs chase their tails because they do not have opposable thumbs, so they can't use a mouse to play solitaire on the computer! That's right, they do it out of boredom. Some experts have said that they do it because they have an itch at the base of their tail, possibly caused by a flea, God forbid, or maybe even ... ahem, well, let's just say a "personal itch" in the area of their little doggy butts. They can't really reach it but they give it the old college try just the same. In the end, does it matter? I mean, it's just so darn entertaining!

Q. Why do dogs chase cars?

A. Dogs chase anything that moves: squirrels, opossums, raccoons, that fake rabbit thing at the dog track. In the wild, wolves detected motion, which meant possible prey, which meant a fine meal with a few friends. So moving cars, or just about anything else that's moving, for that matter, bring out that prey drive in a dog. To a dog, chasing a car is no different than chasing a small animal; it just presents a larger and faster challenge.

But then again, maybe he just wants to come along with you for a ride!

Q. Why do dogs growl at some dogs but not others?

A. Dogs are individuals, so this answer would depend upon the dog. Dogs communicate in many ways, some of them verbal, like barking, snarling, or growling, but many of them nonverbal. Some of the nonverbal clues we pick up from a dog's body are fear, friendship, anger, anxiety, and aggression. The body language of dogs can be very dramatic, as when a dog snarls, raises his hackles (the fur along the back of his neck), or lunges with teeth bared. Other clues can be very subtle. They can be so subtle, in fact, that we can't even see or recognize them. It's possible that your dog could be picking up clues from the other dog. If the other dog is frightened, angry, or not well socialized, your dog will pick up on that fact long before you or even the other dog's owner will. He may decide to exploit that and begin growling and putting on a big act for the benefit of the other dog.

If the other dog is very confident and amiable, your dog won't bother with the act.

Kerry Lake, former breeder of champion Newfoundlands and Bulldogs, says, "While I am walking a Bulldog on the street, I notice that just the sight of him with his sour mug, strong gait, and look of determination will cause the other dog to put on the tough-guy act. This almost always happens with the Bulldogs but never with the Newfoundlands." Sounds a little like profiling to me.

Q. Why do dogs lick their privates?

A. Because they can, goes the old joke. But really, there are a variety of reasons for this behavior. Licking could be more than simply self-gratification. Some of the other reasons dogs lick their genitals are:

* **Cleanliness**—They want to get all the urine or fecal matter off of themselves because they like to be clean (some breeds and individuals more than others). Call these the "petrosexuals."
* **Enhanced odor**—Wetting causes the smell of anything to become more pronounced, and this is

particularly so with dog genitals. Some dogs may want to appear to be more odiferous in order to develop or increase their status in the pack.

* **Obsessive/Compulsive Disorder**—This disorder isn't limited to people. In dogs it can sometimes manifest itself as excessive licking. When a dog is licking his genitals in such a way that it is causing redness, swelling, or bleeding, it's time for a visit to the vet.

Q. Why do dogs hump other dogs or people's legs?

A. This is a very common practice. According to an article published on Petplace.com by Dr. Nicholas Dodman, "one out of every three neutered male dogs and the occasional neutered female still engage in humping." To the casual observer, humping may appear to be a sexual behavior, and oftentimes, it is. However, the dog is not exhibiting this behavior in an attempt to mimic canine copulation, it's more of a show of dominance. Dr. Berkenblit says, "It could be that there is a bitch in heat somewhere nearby, and the dog is acting out on any dog that happens to be around because he is responding to that stimulation. Aside from that, serotonin, a brain chemical, plays a role in this behavior, so it could be purely a form of masturbation. The dog may be asserting dominance, which is related to sexuality because in the wild, the dog that is the most dominant gets the female in heat. So, it becomes about rank and status."

So why would a female dog hump? All animals begin with the same blueprint, which is female. That's why human men have nipples. Each gender has the potential to exhibit behaviors ascribed to one or the other gender.

When a dog humps a person's leg, or another dog for that matter, it's his way of saying "Mom likes me best!" or something of that nature. Basically, he is elevating himself in the pecking order, so to speak. I think it is more of a little-dog thing. There are no statistics to bear this out that I know of, but as a humane educator, I am asked this question all the time, and it is almost always asked by someone who has a small dog. Big dogs don't seem to have the need to exhibit this behavior as much; their size is enough of a deterrent to anyone who may be thinking they are superior to the dog. In their mind, they have nothing to prove. Little dogs, however, may be afflicted with something akin to the Napoleon complex, so they hump away. A Chihuahua can't go out and buy a big speedboat, so he'll hump someone's leg to show what a big shot he is.

Q. Why do dogs hump inanimate objects?

A. Some experts believe that dogs hump out of sheer joy. Former breeder Kerry Lake puts it this way: "It could be any object that strikes his fancy at the time the dog is overjoyed about anything . . . you gotta think DOG. Some objects just smell so good to them, and we can't smell it at all. It could be the oils used on them; it could be that a dog once peed on it at some time."

Dr. Berkenblit agrees with that theory, but adds that humping inanimate objects could also be a way of satisfying an itch or irritation in the genital region—and if it occurs on a regular basis, a trip to the vet is in order. Berkenblit also points out that "Certain behaviors, humping included, can start for reasons such as itching but then continue out of sheer habit. A dog may have done it to satisfy an itch, or because he or she derived pleasure from it, but then the behavior continued out of a sense of habit."

So how do you stop the behavior? After checking for an underlying condition and ruling out any physical problems, the best thing to do is simply distract the dog. If the dog is humping a person, another dog, or a thing, and he is becoming a nuisance, simply distract him without punishment. Remember, to him, it's not really social malfeasance; it's a dog thing and a natural thing to do. We cannot punish them for acting on an instinct. If it's not bothering anyone or another dog, there is no reason to put a stop to it.

Q. Why don't dogs lick themselves for cleanliness like cats do?

A. Dogs love malodorous, offensive goop. They will roll in it and then jump happily onto your bed. They like to cover themselves to mask their own odor if they do not want to be detected, or to enhance their own odor if they want to advertise their presence. Bathing themselves like cats do would defeat that purpose. Furthermore, a dog's tongue is not designed for bathing as is a cat's prickly, sandpaper tongue. However, there are exceptions to every rule. Greyhounds are known to be fastidious and clean dogs who actually do lick themselves to keep clean. Whippets, Siberian Huskies, Italian Greyhounds and, surprisingly, Dalmatians, are all breeds that are commonly thought to be self-cleaning dogs.

If you pick up a starving dog

and make him prosperous,

he will not bite you; that is the

principal difference between

a dog and a man.

—Mark Twain

3

EDUCATED GUESSES:
THINGS DOGS DO AND WHY
WE THINK THEY DO THEM

Q. Do dogs have the ability to exhibit facial expressions?

A. According to Dr. Lorraine, dogs do have the muscles that are necessary to exhibit facial expressions. It's doubtful, however, that they use facial expressions like we do. Body language is so important to dogs, but as far as using facial expressions to show disgust, happiness, or anger, it's hard to say. Even though they have the muscle structure, they probably don't have the attendant, necessary intellectual ability. Of course, most of us who share our homes with dogs have seen "the guilty look" or a look of surprise or fear, so there is reason to believe that they show facial expressions. That could be just our interpretation of what they are doing; we can't truly know what emotions give rise to the expression.

Even though dogs can't really smile the way we do, they understand when we smile. It's only because dogs have been around this behavior all their lives that they can understand us. We have benefited from the relationship as much as they have, so it's to both our advantage to understand one another.

Q. When a dog pees on the bed, is he being spiteful?

A. Dogs are never spiteful. It's simply not in their nature to be spiteful. Dogs know good and well that they've got a good thing going hangin' out with humans, and they are not about to mess it up. In order for us to believe that dogs do things out of spite, we would have to then conclude that they can also feel jealousy, envy, and vengefulness. Hierarchical mentality, which is a pack dynamic, disallows these emotions. A pack could not survive if there were ongoing battles for control, so dogs have the enviable ability to accept the adage "it is what it is." While we may look at our neighbor and wonder "Why does that rat bastard get to drive a red Corvette, date a supermodel, and travel the world?" dogs simply don't have the ability to contemplate why one dog in the pack is the alpha and the others all bow to his or her will.

A dog's level of intelligence and emotion is about that of a two- or three-year-old human. Does a toddler have the capacity to do things out of spite? It's doubtful. Even if you caught your dog out smokin' rawhide with his raggedy friends and grounded him for a week, he could not and would not be able to form the intent necessary to perform an act of spite.

So why does a dog pee on the bed? Professor of animal sciences Susan Helmink notes that dogs tend to prefer absorbent substances to pee on (such as grass as opposed to slate). The reason for this is so they don't wet their feet from splashing or pooling urine. So if they are not well housetrained they may see the bed as an absorbent alternative. "I imagine that it could also be similar to cats urinating on the bed—if a dog is hurting when he pees (i.e., has a urinary infection or some other illness), he may associate the pain with the location and try different areas to see if that helps the pain go away."

Susan also observes that a dog's concept of urine is in direct contradiction to our own. She says, "The interesting thing about spite is that the dog would have to know that we find their urine offensive. Since they have little to no understanding of why we do the things we do, our preferences or our motives, it's a stretch for them to make those connections. (Hey, we pick up their poop and bring it home—does that mean we like it?) Even if we get mad, they still don't know that their specific behavior is what made us mad."

It's for just this reason that professional trainers get so nuts when people think that rubbing a dog's nose "in it" is an approved and effective housebreaking tool. It most certainly is not. Experts always tell new dog owners that they absolutely, positively *must* catch their dog in the act and correct him while he is, shall we say, assuming the position. If you do find that your dog has left a mess on the bed, or anywhere else you don't want it, the best remedy is to roll up a newspaper nice and tight and give yourself a few good whacks on the head with it, because you really should have been watching him.

Q. Can dogs be gay?

A. Do you know the fascinating story of Roy and Silo? These two male penguins living in the Central Park Zoo in Manhattan were very devoted to one another. They even performed what anthropologists call "sexual behavior" with one another, refusing any female companionship. Eventually, zookeepers gave an egg to this "gay" couple to see what would happen. They did just fine. They both played their respective parts, sitting on the egg, and helping one another. The egg hatched, and together they raised the little one. A lovely little family.

Researchers are finding now that there is a part of the brain of homosexual individuals that is markedly different from that of heterosexuals. This means that there may be a genetic reason why some people are gay. There is no reason to believe that this same genetic code cannot be present in other animals. We see that happen in other primates: not gorillas, but chimpanzees, and very much so in bonobos (pygmy chimpanzees). "I wouldn't be surprised if they find that same genetic aberration in dogs," says Dr. Lorraine. "They haven't found it yet, but I don't think they are really looking for it. Of course, if they find this genetic mutation in animals that proves a 'gay gene,' then they can't say that it is there in dogs but not in humans. I have personally seen an unusually close relationship between two male dogs or two female dogs that is much, much closer to a sexual relationship than platonic. They are not having sex, but they share a real closeness. But since we are spaying and neutering a lot of pets, we are, in essence, rendering them genderless anyway. Since humans can be gay, I would say it can be so in dogs too."

Q. Why would a dog prefer the toilet for drinking when he has a fresh bowl of water?

A. Some veterinarians theorize that it's because the toilet, and the bathroom in general, smells a lot like the dog's human. To a dog that's a good thing, and since they don't understand plumbing and fecal matter and E. coli and all that stuff, they figure, "What the heck, why not go to a place that smells comforting?" Anything that smells like the person he loves is a good thing to a dog. Anything. There's a possibility as well that the water in the toilet is colder and fresher than the water sitting out at room temperature in the dog's bowl. Some people leave their dog's water out for days, so it becomes warm and full of muzzle-and-floppy-ear-induced debris. The toilet, however, is refreshed several times every day.

Another explanation could have to do with the material from which the dog's water bowl is made. Plastic water bowls, researchers have discovered, leach chemicals from the plastic into the water and make the water taste funny. Dogs may be more sensitive to the taste of the plastic in the water. That plastic, by the way, is somewhat toxic, so veterinarians encourage the use of glass, ceramic, or stainless steel instead.

Finally, it could just be the dog's preference. There are some cats who only drink water from a dripping faucet just because they prefer to do so. It's possible that dogs have their inclinations as well. Dogs drink by curling their tongues into the water and scooping it up. Dogs who like to drink from the toilet may be more comfortable with the water at that height rather than on the floor, because it's easier to get to and they don't have to bend down as far.

In any event, a lot of dogs all across America must be doing this because vets get this question from their clients all the time. But is the toilet bowl a safe alternative to the water dish? Says Dr. Lorraine, "There is always the possibility of becoming sick from drinking from the toilet bowl. All animals, humans and nonhumans alike, poop out *E. coli* and salmonella at some time or another. Some of that nasty stuff can hang around even after the toilet has been flushed, so your dog could possibly contract it." Makes sense. But it's not the rogue bacterium that worries Dr. Lorraine; it's the stuff we put in the bowls to keep them gleaming white. Those little blue chemical cakes and bleach additives can kill your dog, so if you're using them, it's really important to keep a lid on things!

Q. Can dogs laugh?

A. Dogs cannot laugh like we can because they don't have the anatomical structure necessary to make laughing noises. But experts agree that dogs can experience amusement. A lot of people believe that we are anthropomorphizing (giving animals human qualities) when we say things like that, but what else do we have to go on? Dogs react to certain situations just like we do. They feel fear, they feel threats, they feel emotions such as loneliness and sadness and even anger, so why shouldn't we believe they can feel amused? Many people report that they have seen their own dogs laughing and playing, but they just don't have the ability to make the sound we do. Dr. Lorraine believes that we should relate to them as we do a two-year-old child. "Pranks and jokes may be over their heads, but they can still feel amusement, happiness, and joy."

Sometimes I will play peek-a-boo with my dog or cat by peeking out from behind a wall from different heights by standing on my tippy-toes or crouching down really low. I asked Dr. Lorraine if they "get" that I am playing with them or if they think that I am just acting very strange. "No, they get that," says Dr. Lorraine. "They get amusement. Dogs may not be able to write poetry, but just like kids, they eat, sleep, and play."

Dancing my version of the Irish jig around my dog is simply a form of play for me and I truly think she "gets" that. She certainly reacts as if we are having fun. She wants to join in and she doesn't run and hide or try to rescue me. Dogs have evolved to be with us, and we have evolved to be friends with them. We have created what they are today, because they are not even close to being wolves and dingoes (wild dogs) anymore. So the answer is yes, dogs can, in their own doggy way, share a laugh with us.

Q. Why are some dogs afraid of thunderstorms?

A. I think that when bad dogs die they will be tethered in a place with hourly thunderstorms and loud, honkin' vacuum cleaners, because I can't think of a worse fate to befall a dog. But then, everyone knows there are no bad dogs! Will Rogers said it best: "If there are no dogs in Heaven, then when I die I want to go where they went." Me too!

I will never forget the time I was listening to an Aerosmith CD, volume properly turned way up high (because, after all, that is the only way to enjoy Aerosmith) when a thunderstorm came up out of nowhere, as they do in South Florida. My little house was the victim of a lightning bolt that made a whole lot more noise than Steven Tyler ever could. The resulting boom was followed by a deafening silence, as every appliance was instantly and permanently terminated. My poor dog sat quivering like the Cowardly Lion going to see the Wizard of Oz, and he was never the same after that.

Most dogs, but not all, are afraid of thunderstorms. It's possible that genetics play a role in whether or not you've got a *brontophobic* (fearful of storms) canine. Just like some people are nervous wrecks and others are calm under the most dire situations, dogs can be born with a proclivity toward nervousness under any circumstances that are new or perceived threatening. The reason could also have to do with the dog's environment. If the dog is a rescued shelter animal (who now belongs, of course, to a hero), he could bring with him a whole duffel bag full of memories of being left outdoors on stormy days and nights. Maybe popular *Peanuts* canine Snoopy was at one time a victim of this maltreatment, leading him to begin his daydream life as an author by typing the famous line, "It was a dark and stormy night. . . ."

A young dog left out in a storm with no mom or human to comfort him would be terrified indeed, and that memory could come to the fore every time the barometer drops or your dog hears the sound of distant thunder. This could be a combination of genetics and environment; an already nervous dog with a memory of a time when he was scared out of his wits.

Many times dogs will begin to act as though a thunderstorm is coming long before it comes because they feel minute drops in the barometric pressure. Dogs may also pick up subtle, or maybe not so subtle, cues from the people in the house. Most people pretty much take storms in stride. But if a human is nervous about an approaching storm, the resident dog will pick up on that nervous energy. He won't know exactly why his human is nervous, and that only adds to the uncertainty and fear.

Often when a dog displays the least little hint of anxiety during a storm, his human will try to comfort him, and the result will be a lot of positive reinforcement such as attention and treats in an effort to distract the poor dog. And what does that accomplish? The dog learns to act scared because it's working for him! He is getting attention.

Loud noises, in general, can be very disturbing to dogs. Nowhere is this more pronounced than in a retired racing Greyhound. These dogs are trained to take off at the sound of a starter gun, so any loud noise will make the adopted racing Greyhound jump and try to run. But trainers didn't *train* Greyhounds to be alert to loud noises; they simply exploited an apprehension already present in dogs. This fear of loud noises is most likely a throwback behavior, when the sound of thunder meant heavy rains and lightning for animals in the wild, or a shotgun blast meant a felled member of a wolf pack. And let's not forget that loud noises can just be very scary! Service dogs and those used for hunting, however, are patiently trained to ignore loud or sudden sounds.

So what can you do for your panicky pooch? The first thing doctors recommend is desensitization therapy; that is, play recordings of thunderstorms over and over again when you are home. Start with the volume on low and bring it up nice and loud over several weeks. Rover will get over his fear of storms pretty quickly. Another tried-and-true solution is to try a few drops of an herbal supplement called "Rescue Remedy," which is available in health-food stores. Just a drop under the tongue or on the flews will calm most dogs. But the coolest therapy of all is something that Dr. Lorraine, a certified veterinary acupuncturist, shared. All dogs have a big, hard knot on the very top of their skulls. Just behind that knot is an acupressure point. If you press your thumb firmly and rub very gently in that spot, it will calm your dog right down. However, the best advice, insists Dr. Lorraine, is to turn on your stereo and ignore the storm. I recommend Aerosmith.

Q. Do dogs dream?

A. Anyone who has ever had the pleasure of watching a dog in blissful slumber knows that without a doubt, dogs dream. We who share our homes, hearts, and lives with dogs see the evidence of it every day and night. We witness the rapid eye movement during REM sleep, and we watch in wonder as they move their legs as if running. Sometimes they even whimper, growl, or bark, conversing with some deep psychological characters.

The issue of dogs dreaming is one of those things about which we must anthropomorphize. That means we have to attribute human qualities to animals because we can't get inside their heads. They are so close to us and we know them so well that we have to believe that when they appear to be dreaming, they are. The canine brain is quite similar to ours, their need for sleep is as necessary as ours, and dogs sleep for all the same reasons we do. There is no reason to believe that their subconscious is working in a way that is any different than ours. Scientists have done studies with dogs in which they have used electroencephalograms (EEG) to determine the brain activity of dogs during REM sleep, and so they know that there is brainwave activity associated with dreaming. Dogs, in their dreams, will react to the pictures they see in their heads while they are sleeping just as they would react were they awake.

Dogs' dreams probably don't contain a lot of dialogue and conversation. In her groundbreaking work, Dr. Temple Grandin, author of *Thinking in Pictures* and *Animals in Translation*, discusses how animals think in pictures, not words, much as do people who are afflicted with autism. That makes sense and leads us to believe that doggy dreams are full of images and memories. Whether or not they discuss their dreams with their therapist is another question. But stay tuned: Can a book on dog dreamers and the people who love them be far behind?

Q. Why does a dog stick his head out of car windows but hate it when you blow in his face?

A. Dogs stick their head out of car windows for the same reason we ride motorcycles or snowmobiles: because the feeling of the rushing wind, the coolness on our face, and the sense of speed are exhilarating. They do it for the sensation of the wind in their fur, odors wafting along the air current, and the excitement of going. Dogs have a wonderful sense of being in the moment and enjoying life to the fullest. Who can deny their dog this extra-special treat?

There are those who claim that flying debris and insects can injure your dog's eyes or sensitive nose. That may be true, but in twenty-odd years of treating animals, Dr. Berkenblit and his colleagues have yet to have one come through the door with such an injury. In theory, it sounds like it may be dangerous; but then again, it may just be one of those things people say. Of course, you could play it safe and buy goggles for your dog. But then, he runs the risk of being the butt of merciless teasing at the paws of the neighborhood dogs. Your call.

FUR FACT

If sticking their heads out of windows is not extreme enough, some dogs have been known to participate in actual sports. At Waikiki Beach, there's a whole group of surfers who have outfitted their dogs with life vests to make surfing "dog friendly." And at Vandenberg Air Force Base in California, there's a Dachshund named Brutus who has made "fleafalling" the stuff of doggy dreams, logging more than one hundred jumps with his owner, Ron Sirull.

Remember that dogs have a wonderful sense of smell and it's probable that the wind carries many delectable scents that overwhelm your dog's olfactory system as he takes in all the fragrances flying through the air. Dogs love a sensual, scent-filled environment, which is why they find this so pleasurable.

So why do they hate it when we blow in their faces? Well, blowing air is not something that dogs can naturally do. Think about things that dogs can and can't do and how it must look to them when we do the simple things we take for granted. It's amazing to them that we can hold things like guitars and vacuum cleaners. Because they don't have opposable thumbs, they can't relate. They hate it when we pat them on the head because dogs don't pat; they hate it when we hug them because dogs don't hug (some may tolerate it, but they don't appreciate the restraining effect of a hug). Any action on our part that is not natural or familiar to a dog is something they are wary of. Blowing in their faces is one of those actions. It could also be interpreted as an act of aggression. You have your face right in his face, which he could perceive as a threat. You are right there, your mouth is open, and it looks like aggression to him. He has two choices: He can either bite you or turn away. So, most dogs will turn away. Some dogs will also snap at you or snap at the air. Of course, it could be that he finds your breath offensive because of the deep-fried onions you had for lunch!

Breed not a savage dog,

nor permit a loose stairway.

—Talmud

MYTHS, SAYINGS, AND TRUTHS: WHAT WE SAY AND WHY WE SAY 'EM

Q. Is it true that some dogs, such as pit bulls, cannot feel pain and love to fight?

A. This is one of the saddest and most persistent of all urban legends. Anyone who believes that pit bulls cannot feel pain is out of touch with reality. First of all, there really is no such thing as a "pit bull." The dog known as a "pit bull" is most closely related to the American Staffordshire Terrier, but can be any combination of any number of breeds including the American Staffordshire Terrier, American Bull Terrier, Bullmastiff, Rottweiler, Perro de Presa Canario, and several others. The breed has been much maligned and misused as moneymakers for people who teach them to fight with other dogs while onlookers gamble on the results. The breed may have been given the reputation of a fighter because they are tenacious and will hold fast once they clamp their jaws onto an opponent. But this is true of any number of the terrier breeds, who are known for their tenacity and determination. "Pit bulls" have a nervous system that is identical to any other dog, or us humans, for that matter, and there is no evidence to suggest that pit bulls cannot feel pain.

"Pit bulls," like any other dog, rely on the pack dynamic to survive. Any animal for which there is a group name, such as a herd of deer, a pod of dolphins, a swarm of bees, a pride of lions, or a murder of crows (I know, that last one is so weird), is considered an animal that must live with others of his kind to survive. Dogs are pack animals (as in "a pack of dogs") and need their pack for their very survival. In the absence of other dogs, we serve as a substitute pack for our household dogs. "Pit bulls" need and want the camaraderie of the pack just as much as any other dog, and so making them fight is not only a crime in most states, but also a crime against nature. These dogs must be severely abused and their spirits broken to get them to act in a way that goes so solidly against their nature.

In reality, the dogs known as "pit bulls" or "pitties" are well known to those who have them in the household as the clowns of the terrier group because they love festivity, they adore their families, are wonderful with the kids they love, and are easily trained because of their superior intelligence. The myths about "pit bulls" should be put to rest immediately, because so many lives are lost and communities destroyed by the violence promoted by a dangerous urban legend. Dogfighting brings with it a host of other problems besides the obvious cruelty to animals issue. At organized dogfights, police often find guns, gambling profits, drugs, and minors in attendance. This contributes to a culture of violence in the community, which hurts both animals and humans in the long run.

Q. Why is one year of a dog's life equal to seven years of a human's life?

A. We have all heard the adage that for every year in the life of a dog, he ages seven human years. Though this formula is not totally accurate, there is reason to believe that dogs age faster than we do.

In the first two years of their lives, dogs age much more rapidly than human children do. This is a throwback to their days in the wild, when they needed to mature fairly quickly so they could defend themselves. There is no exact formula to figure a dog's age in human years, but there are some universally accepted theories. For example, a six-month-old dog is believed to have the same maturity level, as measured in its ability to survive and figure things out, as a ten-year-old child. To be sure, a six-month-old puppy will constantly test his limits, just like a prepubescent child, often with similarly nerve-wracking results. And a twelve-month-old dog is comparable to a human at fifteen years. At the age of two, a dog is considered to be at a similar stage in his relative development as that of a twenty-four-year-old human.

Dr. Berkenblit says you can get pretty close by using a simple formula: For each human year up to age two, your dog ages about ten years. After age two, he ages about four to five human years for each year of his life. Using this formula, an eight-year-old dog would be about fifty-five in human years. The mythic number seven mentioned earlier probably came about as an average, because it does take some time and effort to precisely figure out the age of a dog in human years. Also, since it's not an exact science, the precision of the formula is questionable. The number seven thus appears to be an average that can relate to all dogs regardless of breed or size.

The size of the dog also makes a difference. The larger the dog, the faster he ages. Larger breeds of dogs, such as Great Danes and Rottweilers, age much more quickly than do smaller dogs. The life expectancy of a Great Pyrenees is only about ten to twelve years, whereas the life expectancy of a Toy Poodle is fifteen to eighteen years. The smaller breeds also tend to remain active in their geriatric years, markedly more so than the larger dogs. You may have heard the statistic that a city dog will live longer than a dog living in the suburbs. However, it is not the culture and sophistication of a city flat versus a big farmhouse that extends their lives; it's simply that city dwellers are more likely to have small-breed dogs than larger ones.

Q. Does sterilization make a dog fat and lazy?

A. As with any myth or parable, there may be a morsel of truth in this one. Although sterilization surgery itself does not directly cause a dog to gain weight or become less active, it may be an indirect or proximate cause if a dog is gaining weight after surgery to remove his ability to breed. Intact (non-altered) male dogs, especially, spend their days running around the neighborhood with just one thought in mind: "Girls, girls, girls!" Their hormones are raging and they are running hither and yon burning lots of calories and getting a whole lot of exercise. It is during this time in a dog's life that he is most likely to run away from home, and then we see his mug shot on some poster nailed to a tree with the caption "Lost Dog." The horny little bastard has run for miles following the scent of a bitch in heat and somehow lost his way. A female dog in heat can transmit pheromones up to six miles! So any male dog within a six-mile radius is going to have one thing on his mind: getting to the sexy little vixen with the raging estrogen levels!

When we neuter a dog, his level of testosterone drops and with it goes his keen interest in female dogs. Since they have no interest in hanging with their hoodlum buddies cruising for chicks, so to speak, they are content to stay home and curl up by the hearth and let you read them a bedtime story. The result is a drop in exercise levels. If the intake of calories does not drop accordingly, then we get a fatter dog. The same is true for the female dogs, though it's not as dramatic because with dogs it is the male of the species who comes a' callin', so female dogs wouldn't be running around as much even if they hadn't been spayed.

There are solid benefits to neutering so even if there is an obesity and change-of-personality risk associated with sterilization, it's a procedure that should be performed on any dog that's not going to be part of a responsible breeding program. A dog who is neutered is a happier dog, less anxious and more content to hang out. He's not apt to run away, so you won't be forced to offer a reward for someone finding him! Also, sterilization cuts down on problems of aggression and/or difficulty in training. Studies show that dogs who are sterilized relatively early (before twelve months of age) have a reduction in their risk of testicular, uterine, prostate, and mammary cancer as well as other diseases, such as pyometra (a disease of the uterus). So don't put off this important surgery; just cut down a little on your dog's food after sterilization or take steps to ensure that he has a lot of exercise. The indirect result of the latter, of course, is less weight on *you* as well!

Q. Can you teach an old dog new tricks?

A. "I think it's comparable to kids and adult humans," says Susan Helmink, a humane educator and lecturer on animal sciences. "When you are young, everything is new and you are eager to take on new things. As we age, our experiences affect how we perceive new ideas, so we are not as motivated or comfortable trying new things. If a dog was trained using negative techniques such as choke collars or physical reprimands, he may not be as receptive to future training, even with positive reinforcement. Another factor may be dogs who did not get a lot of opportunities to learn when they were young. Perhaps they were very sick or isolated in the backyard or raised without a mother and littermates, so it's understandable that they might have more difficulty learning in the future because they never learned how to learn."

Liz Baranowski, director of humane education for the Pasadena Humane Society in Pasadena, California, has a slightly different perspective on this issue: "The way I see it, if you want to teach me a new trick it has to be worth my time and effort," she says. "To get out of doing something new I have lots of tricks, which I learned while aging. I bet the same is true for dogs. If over the years the dog has learned that humans do not always 'pay up,' then new tricks are hard to learn. So in those cases, it could indeed be very difficult to teach an old dog new tricks."

Once again the experts have spoken, and once again it all boils down to this one fact on which all experts agree: All dogs are individuals and all dogs have their own individual tastes, temperaments, and training plateaus. So go ahead, try to teach that old dog a new trick. Get back to us on that, will ya?

Q. If a dog does not have a cold, wet nose, does that mean he's sick?

A. Dogs' noses are complicated little tools that perform a myriad of services and functions. One of those functions is to keep said dog cool by hydrating the air that passes through his nose so that there is an exchange of air that is fresh, cool, and moist. The inside of the nose is lined with mucous membranes. These membranes need moisture for good health so they can perform their function, which is to catch debris and germs and all kinds of funky stuff before it reaches the lungs. Think of the inside of a dog's nose like those adhesive lint rollers we use on our clothes. Our noses work in much the same way, but the design and structure of our schnozzes helps keep moisture in, whereas a dog's anatomy makes it difficult to retain moisture. The canine snout is great for isolating and sniffing things out, but in order to make it so efficient the nostrils are necessarily straight and open to the air, so they need that added moisture to keep out all the bad stuff and keep the mucous membranes clean and healthy. The "wetness" is a mixture of mucus and saliva, but it starts out as mucus. The dog will lick his nose a lot and the saliva acts as a mucolytic (a substance that thins mucus).

Sometimes a dog's nose will even drip, and that's normal too. The wetness keeps the nose clean and well hydrated so that the nose doesn't dry out, which would cause the mucous membranes to dry out as well. Dogs, during a single day, will go from a cold wet nose to a warm wet nose to a dry cold nose to a dry warm nose at various times and degrees throughout the day, depending on the ambient factors. If there are breezes, if they are indoors or out, if they are in air conditioning or overheated air, their noses will react accordingly. It's just as with contact lenses; the ambient factors sometimes determine whether you need to add eye drops or the eye is well hydrated on its own.

"People call me all the time and say 'the dog's nose is dry, can you come right away,'" says Dr. Lorraine. "And they really believe that it is true. Like all old wives' tales, there may have been some particle of truth; maybe five hundred years ago someone had a dog who always had a cold, wet nose, and just before he died his nose was warm and dry, and so that's how the rumor got started."

The axiom that "A cold, wet nose in the palm of your hand can cure anything" is so true. Cold noses warm our hearts every day in so many ways!

Q. Is it true that a dog's mouth is cleaner than a person's mouth?

A. All animals have a built-in immune system that helps them fight pathogens. Predators, especially, have an efficient germ-fighting saliva that will defend the body when they eat carrion or diseased prey. The saliva does, in fact, have some antibiotic properties. Human saliva does, as well. Canine saliva, however, is much more acidic than ours, which makes it inhospitable to bacteria. So in a sense, it is true that a dog's mouth is cleaner than ours, but where they have about a thousand bacteria per square inch we may have 10,000 in the same area. So, it's cleaner, but it's not clean.

Some silly folks will use this information to avoid taking an injured dog to the vet, the rationale being, "Hey, if he were in the wild he wouldn't be getting medical care, he'd lick it and keep it clean himself." This is never a good idea because of the resident bacteria in the dog's mouth. So for every drop of antibiotic property the wound is getting, it's also being lathered with harmful bacteria. It's far more effective to just give the antibiotic, which doesn't contain the added bacteria. A visit to the vet is always a better choice.

Q. What do we mean by the "dog days of summer"?

A. Astronomers are furiously raising their paws and wagging their tails because they know this one! This particular saying comes from ancient times and ancient galaxies. Back in the day when there were no city lights to dim the night sky, people would look up and see the stars laid out in a seemingly random pattern. So the creative, right-brained, artistic ones would connect the stars, like connecting dots, and find that by painting imaginary lines between the stars, they could form a picture in the sky. Depending upon the peoples of the culture doing the fantasy sky painting, these pictures sometimes took on the form of animals. Ancient Asians saw it one way, Europeans another, and Native Americans still another. Eventually, the constellations were determined and christened. For example, Taurus resembles a bull; Gemini, the twins. And the constellations

Canis Major (big dog) and Canis Minor (smaller dog) represent Orion's two hunting dogs. More current legend has it there's one up there that makes for a perfect Snoopy in the yet-to-be-discovered Peanuts Galaxy!

Anyway, the largest of all the stars in the Canis Major constellation is Sirius, which is also called the "Dog Star." Sirius is the brightest of all the stars. In summer, Sirius appears to rise and set with the sun, giving the impression that it is a sort of solar Mini-Me, mimicking the sun's actions. For twenty days in the latter part of July, especially, the Dog Star rises and falls in perfect unison with the sun, creating the illusion that it is, indeed, responsible for hot summer days. Thus, the "dog days of summer" are named for the dog star of summer, Sirius. Let's all celebrate with a resounding medley of "Twinkle, twinkle little doggy in the window."

FUR FACT
Statistics show that women are more likely to give their dog a human name, such as "Toby" or "Tabitha" (my dog's name!) whereas men are more likely to go for non-human monikers such as "Prince/Princess," or "Duke."

Q. Where does the saying "raining cats and dogs" come from?

A. Some say that it started back in the early 1500s, when people made their dogs and cats live outdoors. During a downpour, the hapless animals would seek cover on the thatched roofs of the cottages in which the people were selfishly snug as a bug in a rug. As the torrential rain fell, the dogs and cats would lose their footing on the roofs and the thatching would give way, causing the animals to come tumbling down, as if from the sky. This seems a little far-fetched to me. Living in a hurricane-prone locale, I have come to the conclusion that any cat of sound mind and body would not climb up to escape the rain; he would seek cover under something low and dense. And I have yet to meet the dog who can effortlessly scramble up onto a roof, let alone during a thunderstorm. These guys are usually cowering in a safe, hidden place, trembling from fear at the thunder and lightning, and trying to stay dry.

Another theory is that in England, the water management program was so shabby that when it rained, there was flooding in the streets and all the dogs and cats drowned. The people would look out their windows and see the animals' bodies floating by and think they dropped from the sky. Really?

Some have proffered that the phrase is steeped in mythology. Being that I have Viking blood sailing through my veins, I favor this explanation. In Viking mythology, cats were believed to exercise control over the rain, while dogs managed the wind. So when it rained, naturally it was the dogs and cats who were responsible.

Jonathan Swift's 1738 *A Complete Collection of Genteel and Ingenious Conversation* included the line, "I know Sir John will go, though he was sure it would rain cats and dogs. . . ." This was the first known written reference to a phrase that is still a part of the vernacular to this day.

Q. Why do we say "sick as a dog"?

A. There are so many phrases in our linguistic tapestry that have to do with animals. We hardly ever stop to think about the origins of "to kill two birds with one stone" or "so big you could swing a cat," and maybe that's for the best.

Actually, we say "sick as" a lot of things. People have said "sick as a frog," or "sick as a mine-dwelling canary." "Sick as a dog" is just one variety of an age-old expression. Throughout history, with the exception of the

Greyhound, dogs have gotten a bad rap. Some people believe that there are verses in the Christian Bible that speak disparagingly of dogs. There are Muslims who maintain that verses in the Koran state that dogs are unclean and Muhammad's followers must avoid them. Though it might be hard for us to understand, some Asian cultures kill dogs for their meat. And, in 2006, much to the horror of the rest of the world, tens of thousands of dogs were killed in the streets just because the Chinese government couldn't figure out a better way to control rabies.

The point is, not everyone in the world has caught up with the Europeans and the Americans, who exude doggy fever to the tune of billions of dollars in sales of dog-related merchandise. Oh yes, we love our dogs! Dogs enjoy a popularity in modern-day America that belies their humble and piteous beginnings. One look into the eyes of a Bassett Hound and it's almost incomprehensible to us that anyone could ever hate dogs. But dogs were once considered lowly, dirty, and cowardly, so the saying "sick as a dog" was uttered in an attempt to make something seem very bad, quite serious, foreboding, and dramatic. Some of these sayings should be laid to rest, because dogs have come a long way since then, and now, it's more likely that you will hear "loyal, true, and loving as a dog," which is so much more accurate.

Q. Is "Fido" really a popular dog's name?

A. A representative of the American Kennel Club said she's never actually seen a Fido registered. She adds, "Maybe I just haven't come across one yet." I asked a few friends around the country who work in animal hospitals, shelters, and training or boarding facilities to check their databases, and nary a one has a dog named Fido in their records. On a Web site that offers the top fifty most popular dog names, "Fido" comes in at number forty-nine!

So where did it come from? Well, had I been able to send a text message to President Lincoln's veterinarian, I would have learned that he did indeed treat a Fido, one Fido Lincoln. A dog of uncertain breeding (a mutt), Fido was yellowish brown with short floppy ears who carried the newspaper home in his mouth and chased his tail to the amusement of onlookers at the barber shop where Lincoln had his hair cut. According to documents in the Presidential Pet Museum, Honest Abe gave Fido away when he and the Mrs. moved to Washington, D.C., upon Lincoln's inauguration. He did so to save Fido, he said, from the terrifying sounds of the city. This was a huge disappointment to Abe's son, Tad, who had come to cherish the scruffy little guy. But the Roll family, who took in Fido, wrote letters to the White House, keeping Tad abreast of Fido's shenanigans until the dog himself was "assassinated" by a drunk who didn't like the way the dog touched him with his paws. This heinous act, astonishingly, took place exactly one year after the Lincoln assassination. Fido, by the way, is derived from the Latin *fidelitas*, a word meaning "faithful."

Q. Is it true that dogs' senses are superior to people's?

A. Animals are amazing, aren't they? It is true that the canine ear is better than that of a human being. So is his nose. His sight is superior in some ways too. But this is not a case of "size does matter," because regardless of the size of the dog's ears or nose, he can hear and smell better than you can! Don't get your dander up, however, because it's really just a matter of compensation. See, dogs do not use their vision in the same way we humans do. They don't have poor vision; it's just different. Let's break it down:

Those Big Brown Puppy Dog Eyes: Those big brown eyes do much more than just melt our hearts, though they do that very well. Dogs have well-tuned peripheral vision; their eyes are on the sides of the head, after all. Their night vision is far better than ours. And while humans are more adept at focusing on a stationary object, dogs detect movement much better than we can.

Also, some breeds have better vision than others. The Greyhound, the Wolfhound, and the Whippet are all examples of "sight hounds." These dogs rely more on their eyes than their noses.

Snout Scents: Humans have approximately five million scent receptors in the old schnoz. Dogs, on the other paw, have an estimated 200 million and beyond. It is believed that the working dogs, especially the hounds, have between 230 and 300 million scent receptors. Dogs have been known to sniff out a single cancer cell, alerting humans to a potential medical threat. They can sniff out a drop of blood that has been dissolved in five quarts of water. Farmers sometimes use dogs to determine which cows are in estrus by sniffing out the hormones. And perhaps most famously, they are used by U.S. Customs and Border Protection, the FBI, and other security agencies to detect the presence of bombs and drugs, and to find lost people and cadavers. Of course, dogs have their own uses for their sense of smell. It allows them to decode pheromones and assess the availability of friendly females or presence of defensive male dogs.

When we see a dog sniffing around, we are watching a real pro at work! He's gathering information in a most reliable and precise manner. His cold, wet nose collects odor molecules floating in the air and then processes them. As they dissolve, these molecules penetrate olfactory epithelium membranes within the dog's nose. Those membranes then send nerve impulses to the olfactory center of the brain. This area of the brain, by the way (in case you are not suitably humbled just yet) is forty times larger in ratio to the olfactory center of a human brain.

My, what big ears you have! A dog's hearing is just as impressive. At both the upper end and the lower end of sound frequency levels, dogs can hear better than we can. And we've all heard of the dog whistle that emits a sound at such a high frequency you have to be a dog to even hear it! Like the eyes, the ears are suited to detecting movement near and far. Dogs with ears that stand erect use them much the same way that cats do. That is, they will rotate them to the direction of the sound in order to hear better. Not even Mr. Spock could do that!

In the end, dog lovers know that it's not the dog's sense of smell, or sight, or sound, that makes him so special; it's his heart and his sense of love and companionship that make him such a necessity in our day-to-day lives.

Dogs have given us their

absolute all. We are the center

of their universe.

We are the focus of their love

and faith and trust. They serve us

in return for scraps.

It is without a doubt the best deal

man has ever made.

—Roger Caras

HOUND HEALTH

Q. Why do dogs "scoot"?

A. Dogs have anal glands located just inside the anus. If you were looking at a clock instead of the inner ring of a dog's rectum, you would see that the glands are located at four o'clock and eight o'clock. The anal glands are responsible for that delightfully heady scent we smell when our dog relieves himself. Have you ever wondered why dog doo smells like, well, dog doo? No matter what the dog eats, or if he is big or small, carnivore or vegan, dog poo all pretty much smells alike. Nature did this so that dogs can leave their scent scattered in their scat. Just as with their urine, dog poo contains odors that are important to other dogs.

But once in a while, these glands become clogged up. The substance inside them has a tarry, oily consistency, like paste. Usually it passes onto the fecal matter and creates no problem. But every so often, the gloppy-gloopy stuff will actually plug up the anal glands. When that happens, it causes an irritating and insistent itch. Dogs alleviate this itch by scooting on the floor, the rug, or wherever they can. The remedy for plugged-up anal glands is called "anal gland expression," which sounds more like the title of a punk-rock aria than a veterinary procedure!

Sometimes, worms will also cause the dog's rectum to itch. But no matter what is causing the itch, the scoot is the dog's only available self-administered method of relief. Itch, scoot, itch, scoot. It's a dog's life.

Q. Is it true that chocolate can kill a dog?

A. It depends on the dog. And it depends on the chocolate. Chocolate contains theobromine, a substance that is toxic to dogs in sufficient quantities. It contains a compound that is very similar to caffeine. Certain types of chocolate, such as baking chocolate, contain more theobromine than do other types, such as white chocolate, milk chocolate, or semisweet (dark) chocolate. So baked goods, such as brownies, pose more of a threat than does a chocolate bunny or chocolate ice cream, the latter of which has very little actual chocolate in it.

One of the reasons chocolate causes illness in dogs is because dogs are not able to metabolize theobromine well. It takes an estimated five to six days for the compound to leave the dog's system. If the dog eats even more chocolate, say, a Hershey's Kiss every day, the level of toxin builds up in the body. It is that buildup that can bring his to a danger zone.

The dog's size also plays a role in how sick chocolate will make him. For a fifty-five pound Standard Poodle, three brownies won't be much of a problem. He may exhibit none of the symptoms. A five-pound Chihuahua, on the other hand, could have a severe reaction with symptoms of chocolate poisoning including increased nervousness, trembling, panting, bloody diarrhea, vomiting, seizure, coma, or indeed, death.

FUR FACT

There are lots of other foods that are poisonous to dogs but do not get as much attention as chocolate. For example: caffeine, onions, garlic, raw eggs or fish, certain root vegetables, grapes, and raisins. Many plants are toxic as well, including daffodils, marigolds, and oleander. For a complete listing of household plants and foods that can hurt your dog, visit *www.peteducation.com* and search under "toxic food" or "poisonous plants."

The rule here is that common sense should prevail. Far too many dog owners become frantic and rush their dog to the vet if the animal happens to eat one measly M&M. It's probably okay to give your Great Dane one Oreo cookie if you really want to, and if your Yorkie happens to find a few crumbs of chocolate cake on the floor, don't panic.

As for me, I think the canine food police came up with this whole thing just as a big excuse to keep dogs from finding out about chocolate, because, once they do, we will have to share it with them. They get our hearts, our homes, and our devotion. They're not gettin' our chocolate too!

Q. Why do dogs throw up when they eat grass?

A. You may be tempted to offer your dog a dollop of Green Goddess salad dressing when he goes outside to eat grass, but it's doubtful that he's going to want it. There are three reasons dogs eat grass. One is that they may be feeling nauseous, and they have come to know instinctively that the substance and texture of grass has the properties to induce vomiting. If they are not feeling well, they intuitively want to throw up, so they will

100

go eat grass to help rid themselves of whatever is in the belly causing the problem. Blades of grass present a gag reflex, like sticking one's finger down one's throat.

The second reason some dogs eat grass is because they just like it. (Hey, maybe they'll take that salad dressing after all!) There are some dogs who enjoy the act of grazing and the taste of grass. But regardless of the reasoning behind its consumption, grass still has that same property of making them throw up. In this second case, there won't really be anything in the vomitus. Many owners become alarmed at the sight of the yellow-green foamy stuff their dog throws up in the yard. That's bile that is stored in the stomach. It mixes with the saliva and the grass and is aerated as it comes up so it becomes foamy, like a lemon-lime smoothie! It assists in the "act" because it's difficult to heave up dry grasses. The presence of the bile foam, and little else, is an indicator that the dog is eating grass for the sheer dietary joy of it and not because he's sick. If he is sick, the vomitus would contain the food that's causing the problem.

The third reason dogs may graze is for the vitamins that are found in the grass. In the wild, dog ancestors ate animals that were mostly herbivores. So even if the wolf himself didn't eat plant matter, the stomach contents of his "dinner" provided some vegetation in his diet. So the rabbit food became the wolf food courtesy of the rabbit that became the wolf food. Get it?

Q. Is secondhand smoke bad for dogs?

A. Secondhand smoke is as bad for dogs and other household pets as it is for people. The reason veterinarians don't see a lot of dogs with respiratory problems caused by secondhand smoke is because diseases such as lung cancer, emphysema, chronic obstructive pulmonary disease (COPD), and other illnesses take a while to take hold. Since a dog's life expectancy is so much shorter than ours, it's very possible that a dog will die before the effects of secondhand smoke begin the disease process. That doesn't mean, however, that the smoke is not making your dog sick. It most surely is, and his lungs and bronchial tubes are becoming inflamed with each exposure. There is also evidence to suggest that dogs hate the smell of cigarettes, since their olfactory receptors are so sensitive, but they don't have the ability to fake dramatic coughing spells and give you dirty looks.

In the award-winning documentary *The Witness*, Eddie Lama describes how he quit smoking when he looked over and saw his pet lying next to him, breathing in secondhand smoke. "I thought, 'he doesn't have a choice,'" says Eddie. Realizing that his pet would probably choose not to breathe in toxic fumes if he could, Eddie quit smoking for the sake of his pet. Now you have another reason to stop too!

Q. How can you tell if a dog is in pain?

A. The thing about pain in dogs is that some dogs are very stoic and they won't show pain or let you know when they are hurting. They will simply suffer in silence. And then there are the drama queens who will stub their toe slightly and scream bloody murder. Dogs are not dissimilar to two-year-old kids. Some will scream out if anything hurts them; others will simply look around to see if anyone noticed and is reacting. If a dog is in pain, he is usually whimpering, crying out, or behaving strangely. It's nothing you can really describe (a condition veterinarians call ADR, which is vet-speak for "Ain't doing right"). He may also want to spend time alone, quietly off in a corner of a room somewhere. Or he could take the opposite method, becoming a "Velcro dog," staying right with you and wanting solace from you, his beloved friend and protector.

Acute pain will also surprise dogs, and if they do cry out, it's that mixture of surprise and pain that will cause them to do so. Often, we see elderly dogs who have been in pain for a long time with arthritis or other bone problems but don't show it nearly as much as a dog whose pain is sudden. It's like elderly humans. You may see them struggling to get out of the chair or out of bed but they are not yelping in pain (well, not normally anyway).

Dogs are at the top of the food chain; they are predators. As predators, our furry friends have the luxury of showing pain, whereas prey animals simply can't. If a prey animal, such as a rabbit or deer, were to be hurt, it knows instinctively to keep very quiet so as not to alert potential predators. But even though dogs are predators, they are also pack animals, and that fact slobbers up the waters just a little. You have to understand pack dynamics to appreciate this difficult concept. If a member of the pack is hurt, sometimes the other members of the pack will go to help him, but sometimes they will just flat-out kill him. Looking at it from the point of view of the dog (or wolf) pack, there is solid reasoning behind these two extreme actions. If the ill or injured member is high up in the pack order, such as a breeding female, perhaps, or a very strong and popular alpha male, the pack will do what it can to help because it's so ingrained in them to preserve the species. But if that pack member is not such a big shot, the pack will slaughter him because he is slowing them down, which makes them vulnerable to other predators.

Q. Is it healthy for a dog to be a vegetarian?

A. American dog owners are very conscientious about their dogs' diet. Some dog-food companies use what is referred to as "Four-d" meats. The meat comes from animals that are diseased, disabled, dead, or dying, so it's understandable that we may want to look at all our options when it comes to feeding our dogs. But dogs are not likely to sit down to a meal of veggie burgers and salad, and even if they could, should they?

Dr. Lorraine, herself a vegan, says, "Dogs are carnivores. You can do it [feed them a vegetarian diet], but I don't recommend it. You have to be very careful and make sure that the individual dog's particular body system can process the non-meat proteins found in tofu or textured vegetable products. Canine bodies are the same as ours except for one major difference, and that has to do with their intestines. As carnivores, dogs' intestines are shorter and as a result, dogs may not get enough protein out of a plant source."

But what do the innards have to do with anything? One of the ways we know if an animal is a carnivore, herbivore, or omnivore, aside, of course, from dietary observation, is to look at its intestines. The length of the intestines has to do with what the animal was meant to consume. It's actually one of the arguments vegetarian activists use. They believe that people were meant to be natural vegetarians because we have long, curvilinear intestines. We have a tough time digesting meat because it takes longer for the meat to go all the way through all those twists and turns and, they say, that's why humans get colon cancer and related diseases—because the meat stays in the colon longer than it should. Dogs' short intestines, and cats' even shorter ones, means those animals were designed to live on protein.

> **FUR FACT**
>
> To get a dog to "shake" (as in shake his body after a bath, not shake his paw), blow lightly in his ear.

When we first began keeping dogs as pets, we fed them what we ate. Dogs were fed the leftovers (giving rise to the term "doggy bag"), including the bones and other leavings from our plates. It's only been since the early 1950s that dogs have been getting their own special food. Dog-food companies sprouted up in response to the demand for dogs as pets after soldiers returned from World War II having served with military dogs and experiencing firsthand the joys of canine companionship.

Dr. Lorraine concedes that there are dogs thriving on plant-based diets, but their owners must be diligent, watching very closely to make sure the dog is not malnourished due to a lack of proper proteins. "You have to constantly be checking their blood work, " she says. "If I have a client who is really motivated to turn his dog into a vegetarian, I will work with them. But they need to be willing to spend the time and effort to make sure their dog is getting everything he needs. I think most people like the convenience of prepared foods and won't want the added cost of routine blood tests and close supervision of the dog's diet."

She believes that an inadequate diet can't be supplemented with vitamins because the nutrients in pill form are not well absorbed. "As carnivores," she explains, "dogs have a much higher need for protein and fat than we do, and they cannot process carbohydrates at all. Feeding a high-carb, low-fat diet leads to fat dogs." The kind of dog food with lots of gravy may be highly palatable to dogs, but it's also highly fattening from all of the carbs it contains.

Dr. Berkenblit is convinced that dogs can live on a vegetarian diet. "There are some high-quality vegetarian dog foods on the market, and I have clients who are earnest about wanting to feed their dogs vegetarian foods. I understand that and will work with the client to ensure that their pet is getting what they need. The vegetarian dog-food companies are careful about putting in the nutrients the pets need. It's expensive, but it can be done."

Both veterinarians agree that a good-quality, brand-name dry food, be it vegetarian or regular, is the best choice for our pets.

Q. Do dogs get cavities?

A. Normal doggy saliva has a protein in it that breaks everything down so dogs don't get cavities. The key term here is "normal saliva," which is the result of a good diet full of meat and fat. So, though dogs are not supposed to get cavities, sometimes they do. The culprit could be the dog food. Dry dog food contains a lot of carbohydrates, so if the food does stick to their teeth, it can cause decay. Veterinarians are seeing more and more cavities due to degeneration caused by sugars, the result of carbohydrates mixed with saliva. This issue with carbohydrates is new with dogs, because dry food has not been around that long. We used to feed dogs meat, bones, liver, or whatever was left over from the evening meal. That's what they ate, and wow, did they love it! But now, we are feeding them these carbohydrates in the form of dry food. Most pet owners are under the impression that dry dog food is better for the dog because it helps to keep their teeth clean. But that can be a double-edged sword when you add in all those sugars. Most dogs have plaque, which is tartar sticking to the teeth, and every once in a while veterinarians will find a rotten tooth during a routine exam. The decay comes from dry food getting stuck up under the gums and causing decomposition. When a veterinarian performs a dental procedure on a dog and finds a cavity, she won't fill it like a human dentist will because it's not simply a hole in the tooth; there's more decay. The tooth is usually extracted.

Q. What is bloat, and why do dogs get it?

A. *Simpsons* fans may remember an episode in which the family dog, a rescued racing Greyhound named Santa's Little Helper, was rushed to the veterinarian for what was diagnosed as a "twisted stomach." This is an actual medical emergency for dogs, and it's life-threatening. A dog's stomach looks like a big kidney-shaped sack. This sack is attached at each end near the top. Think of a hammock, with the hammock being the stomach and the tie-ups being the esophagus and the intestines. The stomach is free to move back and forth. If a dog has a meal—and it doesn't even have to be a very big meal—he has weight at the bottom of his stomach (a person in the hammock). As he is running, the stomach can actually start to swing (like the hammock), and can swing so much that it flips over. Here's where the hammock metaphor stops, however, because if you were in a hammock, you would tumble out. But the stomach is enclosed, so the contents are in there but the tie-ups are twisted so that the digested food cannot leave the stomach. It wouldn't seem that there would be so much empty space within the abdominal cavity, but in dogs, especially big dogs, there is.

The stomach is not that big, but it needs room all around it to expand when it gets full. Dogs with big chests, such as Rottweilers and Great Danes, have a huge rib cage, and even though the stomach is not located in the actual chest, the big rib cage extends far back on the dog's body, creating a cavity inside.

During digestion the stomach releases bacteria, and the by-product of the working bacteria is gas. It normally passes out of the body (flatulence), but now it can't. As the bacteria continue to produce gas the stomach gets bigger and bigger and begins to bloat. The medical term for bloat is "gastric dilation-torsion." The only remedy is surgery, and it must be done immediately because the dog can die within an hour or so if not treated. The doctor will surgically open the abdomen, flip the stomach back over, and the dog is fine. The gas passes out and all is well again. However, once that connective tissue has been stretched, it's very easy for it to happen again. So veterinarians find it necessary to tack the stomach to the sides of the abdominal wall to prevent a recurrence.

The symptoms are easy to spot. A dog will act like he is in pain, will try to vomit or defecate, but will be unable to. The most common sign is that the dog's belly just looks bigger than normal, feels firm and taut to the touch and appears bloated. It's hard to miss. Thankfully, this is one affliction that humans cannot experience because of our anatomy. For us, what goes in, goes down and out. To avoid bloat in your dog, it's best to feed him many small meals instead of one big meal, and never let him run directly following any meal.

Q. Can humans catch a cold from a dog and vice versa?

A. The short answer is no. According to Dr. Lorraine, "There are a few diseases, like E. coli and salmonella, which are both bacterial infections, that can cross species. The common cold is caused by a virus and there are very few known viruses that can transmit from animal to human. However, dogs can get viruses that are similar to the cold virus (coryza), such as the calicivirus, adenovirus, parainfluenza, reovirus, or canine herpes virus. Viruses can and do mutate, so there may come a day when you have to share your NyQuil with your Newfoundland, but for now, the common cold is a human thing, so our dogs are safe."

That's not to say that there are no zoonotic viruses (that is, communicable to both humans and non-humans). HIV is one that researchers believe originated in monkeys, and of course we are all atwitter over what may or may not be an emergency with the bird flu, which is also viral. "SARS (severe acute respiratory syndrome) was first identified in a civet cat, a member of the mongoose family," says Dr. Lorraine. "But the animals didn't have any obvious symptoms; they appeared to be unaffected as the virus jumped from one to the other."

No symptoms? So that means if you are feeling well you may actually be very sick?

Anyway, the short answer is that you can't catch a cold from your dog, and vice versa. There are, however, plenty of other zoonotic diseases that humans and canines do share. Rabies is, of course, the most well known of these diseases, but there are parasites that can be passed from dog to human as well. These may be internal parasites, such as tapeworms or giardia, or external parasites, such as fleas and ticks. So go ahead and share that glass of Dasani with your hound because internal parasites require fecal-to-mouth exposure and fleas and ticks simply jump from dog to human.

If a dog will not come to you after having looked you in the face, you should go home and examine your conscience.

—Woodrow Wilson

6

AMAZING FEATS

Q. How do dogs detect cancer, heart attacks, and seizures?

A. In his best-selling book, *The Angel By My Side,* Mike Lingenfelter writes lovingly of the rescued dog that rescued him in return by alerting him to imminent heart attacks. His dog, Dakota, would place his paws firmly on Lingenfelter's chest and stare intently into his eyes. At first, Lingenfelter did not interpret this behavior, but after suffering several heart episodes immediately following Dakota's unusual display, he figured out that his dog was alerting him to an impending occurrence involving his heart. He offers several theories on how this could be. Among them are the dog's heightened sensitivity to nearly imperceptible changes in body rhythm, muscle tension, electrical impulses, or an unusual odor. Of the phenomenon, Lingenfelter wrote:

No one taught Dakota this behavior, he learned it himself. And I, of course, had no idea he could ever do such a thing. I had no idea that any dog could do this, and apparently neither did any of my healthcare people. Dakota watched me suffer through hundreds of angina attacks, from the time he came to be with me, and I think that he finally just put everything together. Maybe he smelled something different about me, or maybe he just sensed that something was "off," but in any case, he was able to make the connection between that and my subsequent painful response. I believed that he wanted to make sure that I was ready for what was coming next.

Once, I was nursing a fractured foot I had sustained while trying to catch a stray half-starved, mixed-breed dog running down the railroad tracks. I twisted my ankle and snapped the bone. I had a removable cast that I didn't wear when I was sitting for long periods reading, writing, or rocking out to Will Smith music videos. My Standard Poodle, Tabitha, has never been much of a slobber hound. Oh, she'll give you a dainty kiss on the chin if you ask her very nicely, but in general, licking is not to her liking. However, all that changed when I took off my cast. She furiously licked the injured foot as if she was trying to wash away the pain, injury, or just bad vibrations that emanated from that foot and not the other. It was truly remarkable.

In his book *What Do Dogs Know?* author Stanley Coren relates a similar story about a Sheltie named Tracy who lived in New York with her human, Marilyn. Tracy had developed an annoying habit of sniffing Marilyn's back whenever she tried to sit down. Then Tracy began to bite an area on Marilyn's back. Marilyn visited her doctor, where she was diagnosed with an aggressive skin cancer, evidenced by a mole that Tracy tried to remove.

Experts surmise that cancer cells cause a tumor to take on a particular smell and that dogs have somehow determined that this odor is associated with a pathologic process. So work is now being done to train dogs to let doctors know when they smell tumors related to breast, lung, prostate, and bladder cancer. Kind of gives a whole new meaning to the words "lab test," doesn't it?

FUR FACT

War dogs were first pressed into service in World War II, when more than 19,000 dogs were donated to the Canine (K-9) Corps. During the Vietnam War, an estimated 3,000 dogs were credited with saving the lives of 10,000 soldiers. "I could sleep at night knowing they were on sentry duty," one soldier reported. "They knew if anyone was coming even in the blackest of nights."

In addition, dogs called seizure dogs are now assisting people who are afflicted with epilepsy, diabetes, or other seizure-producing illnesses. Some seizure dogs are trained to detect and alert to an oncoming seizure, while others are trained to assist during a seizure. Scientists don't have a solid answer as to how the dogs know when a seizure is imminent, but suggest that nearly imperceptible changes in the person's body language, brain impulses, or body odor may be responsible. You just can't fool that superior canine schnoz, and when that is coupled with intelligence, dogs can put two and two together. That's truly an amazing feat.

Q. When did we first start employing dogs to help the blind and disabled?

A. There is a popular joke making its way around the Internet about two guys who try to sneak into a bar with their dogs.

First guy says, "Damn it's hot. Wish I could go to the bar and get a cold beer, but the sign says, 'No Pets Allowed,' and I can't leave Sebastian alone on the street."

Second guy says, "We can get in, watch this." Second guy dons a pair of dark sunglasses and, dog in tow, walks into the bar. The bartender sees the dog and says "No dogs allowed!" The man says, "But he's my Seeing Eye dog!" The bartender says, "Oh, that's fine then, what'll ya have?" The first guy, seeing his friend's ploy working, dons his own sunglasses and proceeds into the bar, Sebastian trailing behind. The bartender says, "Hey! No pets!" First guy says, "But he's my Seeing Eye dog!" The bartender looks doubtful and replies "They don't make no Chihuahua Seeing Eye dogs!"

The guy is undaunted and blurts out, "You gotta be kidding! They gave me a Chihuahua?"

Anyway, Seeing Eye dogs, also known as Guide Dogs or Leader Dogs, depending upon the school from which they graduated, have been around since just after World War I. They won't drive the getaway car or tell you honestly if your pants make you look fat, but they can do a whole lot of other things.

The story of Michael Hingson and his guide dog Roselle is a most famous and oft-told story of modern-day guide dog heroism. It's the story of how Roselle guided Michael to safety while they were working in the World Trade Center on September 11, 2001, and the world tumbled down around them. Despite Michael's dismissal of Roselle in an effort to allow her to save her own life, Roselle steadfastly and successfully guided Michael down countless flights of stairs and amazingly, saved both their lives.

But where and when did we begin employing dogs as assistants to the blind? After World War I, there were many soldiers who had been blinded in the line of duty. Work began at a school in Potsdam, Germany, to teach German Shepherd Dogs to assist those who had lost their sight. The school's purpose, however, was only to help blind soldiers, without a direct benefit to the general public. And so the program ambled on and almost fizzled out until an American living in Switzerland took a keen interest. A breeder of German Shepherd Dogs, Dorothy Harrison Eustis, is credited with recognizing a movement afoot to train dogs to help people. She is credited with bringing the program to the United States in 1927. In this country it took on a larger focus, that of helping all blind people, not just soldiers.

Her first student was "Buddy," a female German Shepherd Dog, who was eventually paired with a young man by the name of Morris Frank, of Tennessee. The rest, as they say, is history. There are about ten accredited schools in the United States that train and place guide dogs, and not all of them use German Shepherd Dogs. Labrador Retrievers, Standard Poodles, and many other breeds have all been pressed into service as guide dogs because they possess the qualities that trainers look for: a willingness to be of service to humans, intelligence, trainability and, of course, really good eyesight.

Seeing Eye dogs were the first to step up to help "differently abled" humans, but since those days in 1927, dogs have been stepping up to perform many other necessary functions for people. We now have service dogs to assist those in wheelchairs or who have mobility issues, and hearing dogs to help the deaf. Canine Companions for Independence is just one of many organizations that help raise and train dogs to perform a wide variety of services such as turning lights on and off, bringing the phone, picking up dropped items, pulling wheelchairs, and so much more.

Dr. Berkenblit has a retired service dog by the name of "Hey Mon." One day, while visiting the clinic, I dropped my sunglasses but didn't know it. Hey Mon not only picked up my glasses, but followed me around the clinic until I noticed him and let him "hand" them back to me. Truly, dogs never fail to amaze me!

Q. Why is a dog credited with the invention of Velcro?

A. Sometime during the early 1940s, Swiss inventor George de Mestral went for a stroll with his dog. Upon arriving home, he found that his dog's coat was littered with those pesky cockleburrs, the kind that get in your dog's feet and you prick your fingers until they are a bloody mess while you're attempting to remove the cockleburrs from the struggling dog. Anyway, de Mestral was a curious fellow and he wanted to understand why these plant-based pods were so tenacious. He placed one under a microscope and looked at it very closely. He saw that each of the burrs had spikes that were curved at the end in a hooklike fashion. This led him to invent a type of fastener that gets its apparent adhesive property from hooks and loops. The word "Velcro" came from the French *velours* (velvet) and *crochet* (hook). What's interesting is that among doggy professionals, a dog who is very bonded with his owner and won't leave his side has come to be called a "Velcro dog," bringing us full circle!

Q. Which is the better predator, dogs or cats?

A. Cats, by far, are the more talented predators. Wolves hunt in a pack, so they need the support and cooperation of other animals to help bring down the prey. Cats, on the other hand, though they may live in a group called a "pride," are stealthier and have the ability to bring down prey one-on-one. Cats can also follow prey up a tree, something that dogs and wolves cannot do. Cats' teeth are made for quick killing; their incisors are curved backwards and they instinctively know to cut through the spinal cord with deadly precision, killing their prey instantly. (This depth and curvature, by the way, is why cat bites are so much more complicated and infectious than dog bites.) Domesticated dogs and cats are no longer required to hunt for their prey to survive, yet cats will still chase lizards, birds, and insects if given a chance. Some dogs, especially those in the terrier group, will also chase down small prey, but it's mostly for sport or to protect (they think) their territory. They get so much pleasure in it, we'll just let them go on thinking that!

FUR FACT

Which is faster, the dog or the cat? Domestic cats have been clocked at thirty miles per hour, but the Greyhound, the fastest dog in the world, can reach speeds up to forty-five mph, making the dog the clear winner!

Q. Can dogs really "smell" fear?

A. Yes. Where there is fear, there are pheromones that are present because of the fear. When an animal, human or non-human, is fearful, traumatized, or anxious, his body releases a pheromone that some experts believe dogs can actually smell. But it's not just the smell of these pheromones that notifies the dog that fear is in the air; it's also body positioning, which gives off delicate and profound signals when an animal is fearful. When a dog smells fear, most of the time he will exploit that by putting on a big show of force. That's why humane educators tell kids to "stand like a tree" and try not to exhibit fear when a dog is charging at them. It's really tough to do, but it works. Think brave thoughts and don't look the dog in the eye.

Q. Do dogs understand English?

A. The question really should be, "Do they understand the spoken word?" Professor of animal sciences Susan Helmink says, "My personal feeling is that dogs can understand the spoken word, at least single words and short phrases. If they didn't, how could they comply with our cues? I believe they pick up on vocal tone, and there are many dogs who respond to a question phrase regardless of the content. But, we have seen that they can pick up on specific words even in a sentence not directed at them." Indeed, I have been on the phone telling my friend I was going to the beach when my dog will suddenly awaken from what appeared to be a deep sleep and is suddenly on his feet, eyes shining, tail wagging, looking at me expectantly: "Did someone say we are going to the beach???"

Helmink cites a study that is causing quite the buzz in the dog world. Researchers conducted an experiment involving a Border Collie by the name of Rico, the results of which were published in a 2004 *Science* magazine article titled "Word Learning in a Domestic Dog: Evidence for 'Fast Mapping.'" During the time he was growing up, his owners—who were also the researchers—taught him more than 200 words. They conducted many experiments to be sure he was actually using his knowledge of the words rather than subtle physical cues from his owners.

In Rico's test, toys were placed in a room separate from the room where his owners were. The researcher then asked Rico to go get a toy—let's say, a ball. Rico complied. Then he was asked to go get a chew toy, and again he complied. Doing this necessitated Rico to scan for the expected item in a room with ten other toys and choose the one that was being asked for. Of forty experiments, Rico got thirty-seven correct. Studies such as this one are not rare, and are probably going on in American households all the time. I know they go on in mine!

Q. Can dogs sense danger?

A. While there can be no absolute, irrefutable proof that dogs have the ability to sense danger, there is plenty of anecdotal evidence to suggest that they do. We know that other animals, especially those that live in the wild, have an acute "sixth" sense that warns them of danger. After the 2004 tsunami in Indonesia, stories abounded of elephants and bats heading for high land before the disaster. While an estimated 162,000 human lives were lost in that tragedy, experts were astounded to find very few wild animal bodies along the coast. So the question is: Because of domestication, have dogs lost the ability to sense danger that we see exhibited by wild animals? It appears unlikely.

In an article about the tsunami, *National Geographic* magazine reported that two pet dogs had stubbornly refused to go on their daily walk on the beach the day of the massive tidal wave. Alan Rabinowitz, director for science and exploration for the Wildlife Conservation Society in New York, reported to *National Geographic* that he believes animals can sense imminent threat because of their ability to discern sudden shifts in their environment, no matter how minute they are or how oblivious we humans seem to be. "Earthquakes bring vibrational changes on land and in water, while storms cause electromagnetic changes in the atmosphere," he said. "Some animals have an acute sense of hearing and smell that allow them to determine something coming toward them long before humans might know that something is there."

But there's more evidence that dogs can detect danger even if it is not a natural disturbance. Witness the guide dog, or the service dog, which uses his powers of discernment to willfully disobey a command given him by his charge. These amazing dogs are taught to understand that the person they are caring for is sometimes unable to make educated decisions. For example, a blind person may give the dog the "forward" command, but the dog may see a car coming or a bicyclist approaching or a change in the level of the road that would cause his companion to fall. In these cases, the dog will use his own judgment and fail to perform an act that would prove dangerous to his human. This is called "intelligent disobedience" and is quite impressive. Other examples of this would be a dog walking on a leash with his owner, who is stopped on the road by a stranger. The dog may pick up subtle clues in his owner's body language that communicate to the dog that the owner is uncomfortable with this person. Dogs read body language very well. After all, among dogs, body language is the primary communication tool.

If you get to thinkin' you're

a person of some influence,

try orderin' somebody else's

dog around.

—Cowboy wisdom

7

BREED BITS

Q. Are Greyhounds faster than all the other dogs?

A. Greyhounds have been clocked at forty-five miles per hour, and are indeed the fastest dog. In a contest of land animals, dogs are second only to cheetahs, who can reach up to seventy miles an hour. Greyhounds are sprinters, however, and cannot keep up that rate of speed for more than a minute or two. It is because of this that Greyhounds have been cruelly exploited in a sport that forces them to live fast and die young. Once the pride of aristocracy and influence, the Greyhound has lost its privileged status and is a mere pawn in the gambling circuit. A scene in an early *Simpsons* episode showed Homer and Bart at a Greyhound race. The dog that came in last was literally kicked to the curb by his owner, a scene not too far removed to reality. Santa's

Little Helper was quickly adopted by Homer and brought home as a Christmas gift for the family.

According to the pro-racing National Greyhound Association, an estimated 5,000 Greyhounds were killed in 2003. This is a sport so cruel it has been outlawed in thirty-five states, thanks to the efforts of advocacy groups such as Grey2K USA.

Q. Are mutts healthier than purebred dogs?

A. In 1994, *Time* magazine published a cover story called "A Terrible Beauty." The article laid out sound and convincing arguments that purebred dogs, more so than mutts, can indeed suffer from a myriad of genetic defects. For example, Cocker Spaniels are subject to a malady known as "cherry eye," in which the bottom conjunctiva (the inside of the eyelid) protrudes outward, exposing the lining of the lower eyelid. German Shepherd Dogs and other large breeds tend to get hip dysplasia, a skeletal condition affecting the femoral head so that the hip is not securely seated in the hip socket. It is well known that there are particular dog breeds that are predisposed to hip dysplasia, but though it is an inherited disease, it's not necessarily congenital. Therefore, the dog will not present with it until he is well past breeding age. This means that the disease can be unwittingly passed from generation to generation.

Dr. Lorraine explains it this way: "Evolutionarily, animals keep traits that are beneficial and lose traits that are anti-survival. When we breed dogs just for looks or conformation, as most breeders do, we ignore health issues that the dogs may have. Thus when we breed, dogs end up keeping the traits for hip dysplasia, cataracts, allergies, cancer, et cetera. When dogs breed naturally, creating so-called mutts, evolution gets to play a hand and dispose of traits that can make a dog unhealthy. Mutts are definitely, overall, healthier than purebred dogs." Giving us yet another reason to avoid the pet store and head for the animal shelter.

Q. Are all Greyhounds gray?

A. Not at all. The name "Greyhound" has nothing to do with the dog's color. Greyhounds come in a wide variety of solid colors and brindles—a sort of brown and black striping—and even the occasional pink and purple paisley print. Okay, I may have made up that last part, but ancient art depicts Greyhounds ablaze with colors, bling, and festooning, so we know that they were very special dogs. The ancient Egyptians first discovered and befriended the Greyhound and used the dogs to hunt other predators, such as wolves and wild boar, as well as large prey such as deer. These dogs were so exclusive that only the ruling classes were allowed to own them. Hence, the name *Gre* or *Gradus* which in Latin meant "first among or greatest hound," which was coupled with the Old English *hund* meaning hound. This ultimately led to "Greyhound." There are some other theories that the first breeding stock of the dog was gray, or that the name "Greyhound" is actually a derivative of "gaze hounds," which is another name for sight hounds. However, the most commonly accepted theory is the Latin mispronunciation.

Q. How did the Jack Russell Terrier get its name?

A. Back in the 1800s in jolly old England lived a man by the name of John Russell, who was well known as a pretentious and showy fellow, a character among the townspeople of Devonshire. Russell was, in fact, a reverend who was irreverent when it came to foxes. He was obsessed with fox hunting and "creating" the perfect dog as a hunting companion and helpmate. Watching the popular Jack Russell Terrier "Eddie" on the TV show *Frasier,* it's hard to believe that this dog's purpose in life was that of a canine hit man, but bred for fox hunting he was. The early versions of this dog were well suited for just that.

Parson John (Jack) Russell worked tirelessly to create a breed of dog that was resolute, flexible, hard working, built for moving fast into deep tunnels, and very daring. He did this by continually breeding small, white, sleek hunting terriers that were exactly fourteen inches in height and between fourteen and seventeen pounds; dogs who exhibited tenaciousness, ferocity with red foxes, and courage. After all, the dog had to take on frightened, angry foxes and raccoons and make it look easy!

Russell looked to the fox when constructing this breed, and concentrated his efforts on molding a

FUR FACT

In 1984 the "Beagle Brigade" became an integral part of security at Los Angeles International Airport and later at Miami International Airport. Officials estimate that they are responsible for some 60,000 confiscations a year, helping to keep insects and bacteria out of our agricultural areas by sniffing the luggage and cargo coming in from other countries.

dog who resembled the fox. The thinking was, "If the fox can fit there, then so must the dog." Being the narcissist that he was, it's little wonder that Jack Russell named the breed after himself, a moniker that served for two centuries.

However, as of April 1, 2003, the AKC officially changed the name of this dog to Parson Russell Terrier, according to the director of education at the Pasadena Humane Society, Liz Baranowski, who studied the breed history. "It appears there was a disagreement about breed standards. The Parson Russell Terrier Club wanted to keep to the original breeding and intent of Parson John Russell, but the Jack Russell fanciers had a different conformation, or standard, in mind. The name change reflects the original breeding standard to conform back to the long, fox-like body instead of a short-legged, stocky dog that the Jack Russell had sort of morphed into."

By the way, that first terrier, the one with the really bad hair who was bred by Jack Russell? His name (I am not making this up) was Trump! I recognize and appreciate the dedication that dog enthusiasts feel for their breeds and breed standards. But I'm

FUR FACT

The first official dog shows were held in England in 1859 with the rest of Europe and America soon following suit. Judges based their criteria on pedigree and appearance. Prior to that, dog shows were nothing more than guys in bars showing off their handsome hounds for all to admire.

afraid that most of us will still think of Eddie, the dog on *Frasier*, no matter what they call the Parson/Jack Russell Terrier. And so it will always be.

Q. Are all dogs good swimmers?

A. Almost all dogs can perform a pretty mean dog paddle if they must, but there are some dogs that cannot swim at all. It really depends on the dog. When we swim, we rely heavily on buoyancy. The less muscle and more fat we have, the more buoyant we are. So a lot has to do with body fat and muscle and the shape of the dog. Think of an arrow going through water compared to a rock going through water. Even if the rock and the arrow both weigh the same, the arrow will go faster because of its shape. Let's take a look at the Bulldog, who has a massive weight with no buoyant properties. This breed has short legs, so there is not a lot of water displacement and they cannot swim. A longer dog has better water displacement. Big dogs like Newfoundlands and Golden Retrievers were bred to be great swimmers, so they have wide bodies and layers of fat and thick hair that traps air, helping to add to the buoyancy. Poodles are also water dogs but they don't have a lot of fat, so for them it's more about conformation (a dog's conforming to the breed standard) and less about weight. Grey-hounds are definitely land animals, as we can see that they have very little fat. These athletes can swim, how-ever, because of their long bodies and long legs, which help keep the water evenly displaced.

One would think that water dogs are a cinch for being great swimmers. But when I moved to Florida from New York in the middle of my senior year, my parents bribed me with my choice of a dog. I chose the Irish Water Spaniel because I'm Irish and I was moving to a beachside city. Well, Patrick was terrified of the water and actually threw up whenever I brought him within fifty feet of the ocean. Once again, it was evidence of doggy individuality winning out over breed profile.

Q. Are some dogs better suited to being "working dogs" than others?

A. Absolutely! Anyone who has ever watched a dog show on television knows that "working" is one of the seven categories, or groups, of dogs.

These groups are the sporting group (you can find them hanging out at Hooters), non-sporting group (they hang out there too, but never pick up the tab), the toy breeds (the ones those skinny celebrities wear), the herding group (most of them go on to become kindergarten teachers), the Hounds (quite the aristocrats), Terriers (from dainty cream-puff Silkies and Yorkies to the bull-in-a-china-shop "pit bulls"), and, of course, the Working group. Dogs in this last group are the salt of the earth, the best of the best, the "look out for your job" dogs.

For this answer, dogs in both the herding and the working group will be considered "working" dogs. It was only within the last few decades that the AKC even added the group "herding." Before that, dogs in both the herding group and the working group were categorized as "working" dogs. The "herding" group came about because there were too many breeds for one group, and so the herding group was created to include those dogs whose job it is to "herd" something, such as sheep.

So just how does one become a working dog? We've carefully bred certain traits into them, or we reinforced behaviors that they offered and we wanted. It's not instinctive for a dog to be a "working" dog, but there is a genetic trait to be of service, to feel needed, and to have a function in life that we have deliberately engineered to pass on from generation to generation. Dr. Lorraine says, "I have a Sheltie (Shetland Sheepdog) that herds us, and her puppy is also herding us. We didn't teach her to do that. She's just doing it." She's doing a job; that is, "herding."

Once upon a time, when Border Collies were being "developed," sheep herders took two dogs who enjoyed working with sheep and bred them, and kept breeding them. The same is true for German Shepherd Dogs and other working breeds. Having intelligence and the trait for herding sheep or meeting any challenges is bred into them.

Susan Helmink, a humane educator and lecturer on animal sciences, adds, "I think this goes back to initial selection for working ability. Before the time when members of a breed looked consistent, people would select the dogs that were best at the job and then breed them. If the job was pulling sleds or carts, they would select the largest and strongest dogs and breed them. So after many generations, common physical traits arose, such as large skeletons, body type, wide chest, et cetera. The same could be said for herding, protection, retrieving, tracking, et cetera. So toy breeds, who were developed as companions, do not have the same working abilities in their backgrounds, while today's other breeds do." This explains why some dogs are better suited to working than others; it was a carefully crafted and carried-out plan to create dogs that could perform a service for us.

Q. How can tiny dogs like Chihuahuas and Pugs be related to big dogs like Irish Wolfhounds and Bullmastiffs?

A. About 40 million years ago, a group called Canidae roamed the earth. All dogs, domestic and wild, are from an original ancestor, which was a member of this group There were many animals in this group, including the wolf, many varieties of jackals, coyotes, African Wild Dog, dhole (a prehistoric, dog-type critter), foxes, and other types of dogs, called the "bush dog" and the "wild dog." Just as humans come from an original ancestor and then people with certain characteristics began breeding together to create entire races, breeds of dogs broke off from that original ancestor in much the same way.

In North America, dogs are descended from wolves, coyotes, and foxes. In Australia, they have descended from dholes and dingoes. In parts of Asia, there are dogs who were the result of a sort of jackal/coyote/bush dog type of animal. So, the gene pool is diverse and varied. However, these dogs did not stay geographically separated forever. In the sixteenth century, explorers brought native dogs with them and left them on foreign shores.

They took new dogs with them when they went back home, giving dogs a world tour and setting the stage for doggy commingling and diversity.

Originally, wild wolves, dingoes, coyotes, and other doglike animals were attracted to human's camps, as they scavenged people's leavings from their meals. Over time, people took in some of these animals as companions—most likely they would find young canines whose mother had died, and take them in. These puppies (wolf, dingo, dhole) were raised with people. As they matured, the ones that stayed placid were kept. If any showed any wild or aggressive tendencies, they were killed or otherwise removed from the camp.

This led to a stock of "domesticated" animals. They were selected by looking to their temperament. They were useful to people in that the dogs could help hunt for food—track it and catch it. Over time, some dogs were born with long hair and some with short hair. People who preferred long-haired dogs would select a long-haired male and a long-haired female and breed them (this is called selective breeding). More often than not, long-haired puppies would be the result. Repeated selective breeding, over time, would produce a population of long-haired dogs. Some individual dogs were better at chasing animals but not killing them. An observant human would recognize this, then select out a male and female that exhibited those traits and breed them. Herding dogs would result. Some individuals would have long legs and thin bodies and were very fast runners. Again, by selecting males and females that exhibited those traits and breeding them, and then breeding only the longest-legged, thinnest-bodied, and fastest progeny, long-legged, thin, fast dogs were bred consistently. Thus the Greyhound was "invented."

Some random dogs had short legs and excelled at killing rodents that followed the humans. By selecting and breeding the dogs with the shortest legs and most intense desire to kill rodents, people "invented" the terrier breeds. Occasionally an odd or unique litter of pups would be born, say, with very short noses. By inbreeding the shortest-nosed male to the shortest-nosed female, short-nosed pups were born. Over repeated breedings of the brachycephalic (short-nosed, pushed-in face) litters, dogs such as the Mastiff were invented. The Pug is most likely a result of the runt puppies of Mastiffs being bred over and over.

Since the age of sexual maturity in dogs is only six months and the gestation period for a dog is only sixty-one days, a generation in canines is only a year or two instead of the twenty to twenty-five years it takes in people, so it does not take as long to create a new "race" or breed of dog. And remember, wolves are not the only wild ancestors; there are also dingoes, jackals, foxes, and a host of others. Dogs and foxes cannot breed now because their chromosomes are incompatible, but maybe there was a time when they could. Also, some species that could have been involved in all this interbreeding may have become extinct over time, and we may never even know if they existed at all.

These varieties of the family Canidae were a diverse and varied group. Some of the modern-day dogs more closely resemble the wolf, while others have a distinct foxlike countenance. Still others have the body type and/or traits of the dingo, the coyote, or any number of these combinations.

In the nineteenth century, people began moving from farms to cities, and they took their dogs with them. Formerly "outdoor" dogs became "indoor" dogs, or house pets. Selective breeding took a whole new direction, with dogs being deliberately bred for their looks and not so much for their purpose. In people

> **FUR FACT**
>
> Lots of dogs bred to be water dogs have webbed feet, including the Akita, Poodle, Chesapeake Bay Retriever, Flat-Coated Retriever, Labrador Retriever, and Golden Retriever breeds, as well as the Irish Water Spaniel, the Portuguese Water Spaniel, and the German Wirehaired and Shorthair pointers, among many others.

and wild animals, evolution is for survival, but in dogs and cats, it is for aesthetics and purpose.

Q. Is there a difference between a mixed breed and a crossbreed?

A. A mixed breed is the result of a whole bunch of different dogs getting together over time. Maybe you have a mutt who breeds with another mutt (maybe we should use the more politically correct "natural dog"). A mixed-breed dog is a dog in whom it is difficult to determine, in most cases, what the foremost breeds are. A crossbreed, however, is a dog who is the offspring of two purebred dogs. The newest fad in designer cross-breed dogs are the Schnoodles, Labradoodles, Golden Doodles, and just oodles of doodles, with new combos coming out monthly. These are dogs whose parents were purebreds, but they themselves are crossbreeds; essentially, intentional mutts. The Schnoodle is the result of breeding a purebred Schnauzer with a purebred Poodle; the Labradoodle is the result of crossbreeding the Labrador Retriever and the Poodle; and the Golden Doodle is the offspring of a purebred Golden Retriever and a Poodle.

In each of these cases, even though they have adorable names and all the celebrities are agog over these dogs, there is no guarantee that each member of the same litter will look alike. The rationale behind creating these Poodle mixes, allegedly, is to give the people what they want! And what they want, evidently, is a dog with the nonshedding coat and intelligence of a Poodle and the temperament of a Labrador/Pug/Bichon Frise/Boxer/Cairn . . . and on and on. Some of these dogs are shedding like crazy, and some of them don't match their littermates at all, which leaves them out in the cold and being dropped off at shelters. In other words, you can buy two Labradoodle littermates at a cost of about a thousand dollars each, and one will shed and one will not. There are no guarantees with dogs that are not the result of careful and responsible breeding.

Q. Are French Poodles really from France?

A. *Das ist ein Deustch hund!* Poodles originated in Germany, not France. They are water dogs, with webbed feet and curly coats perfect for retrieving fowl in the water. The fancy-schmancy coat actually serves a purpose. The balls of fur about the joints and chest were meant to keep the dog's internal organs and bones warm, while the clipping of the rest of his body was an effort to make him more streamlined and lessen the resistance as the dog swam. The name "Poodle" is derived from the German *puddeln* or *pudel,* which means "to splash." Poodles got the misnomer "French Poodle" when the French became smitten over them the way America embraced the 1965 Ford Mustang! The Poodle, though not a native of France, is nevertheless the official dog of France. Vive la Poodle!

Q. Who was the most popular First Dog in history?

A. Fala, the beloved Scottish Terrier of President Franklin D. Roosevelt, was the most popular First Dog because he was very much in the public eye, going everywhere the president did. The public came to anticipate his appearances, and loved him as their own. According to the Franklin D. Roosevelt Presidential Library, Fala even needed to have a secretary appointed to answer the thousands of letters he received from people and dogs alike. Upon the moment of President Roosevelt's death, witnesses say, Fala ran out the door and up the hill, barking and chasing something that only he could see.

Could he have been following the spirit of the departed president?

Q. Is there really such a thing as a hypoallergenic dog?

A. Okay, let's get one thing really, really clear. There is no such thing as a hypoallergenic breed of dog. There has never been a hypoallergenic breed of dog, and the new doodle dogs are not hypoallergenic. Got it? Good.

Now please turn your attention to the following list of hypoallergenic dogs:

* Soft Coated Wheaton Terrier
* Bichon Frise
* Bedlington Terrier
* Schnauzer
* Poodle
* Portuguese Water Dog
* Irish Terrier
* Wire-Haired Fox Terrier
* Havanese
* Maltese
* Kerry Blue Terrier
* Basenji

* Italian Greyhound
* Chinese Crested
* Mexican Hairless
* Doodles: Labradoodles, Golden Doodles, Schnoo-
  dles, and so on

Confused? So are a lot of folks, doctors, veterinarians and dog experts included. There's good reason for that. Most of these dogs have a fur coat that is made of a substance closer to hair than fur. These dogs have locks that grow and grow, and must be cut like a human's hair, and they do not shed like a regular dog's coat. Many of these dogs are living quite comfortably with people who were once told to never attempt dog cohabitation.

Here's the thing about hypoallergenic dogs: There is no hard-and-fast proof that hypoallergenic dogs exist, but there is an abundance of circumstantial evidence to suggest that they most certainly are out there, walking among us, living happy and productive lives.

Folks who have these breeds will swear upon a stack of bibles and they wholeheartedly believe, with the utmost certainty, that there is such a thing as a hypoallergenic breed of dog. Are these dogs real or are they mythical creatures, like J. K. Rowling's hippogriff?

There is a mistaken belief that it's the dog's fur that brings on allergy symptoms. Most likely, however, it is their dander, urine, saliva, and oils in the skin that are the culprits. Long or short strands of fur are not making their way to your immune system. It is the minute, microscopic entities that are causing the trouble.

Dander is similar to what we call dandruff. If you were producing it, you would employ a dandruff shampoo to reduce the flaking. There are dog shampoos that are also effective against dander. Dog dander is composed of microscopic flakes of dead skin being sloughed off our dogs. It normally is a perfectly harmless and natural biological occurrence, but for allergy sufferers, it is anything but harmless. It is downright toxic. The dander can become airborne, or it can settle into carpeting, upholstered furniture, linens, and clothing. It sticks to walls and draperies and stuffed animals and can be almost impossible to get rid of. Even if we do rid our homes of dander, our friends who have dogs will happily share theirs when they come to visit.

A quick and easy way to determine if it is the protein in the saliva and not the dander that is bothering you is to let a dog lick your hand or arm. If you are allergic to saliva, a rash will break out where the dog's tongue has been. Dogs do not lick themselves routinely, but they probably will lick any willing humans standing around because they like the saltiness and oils in our skin. If it is the dander, you may be in luck because the dogs listed above are considered non-dander or low-dander-producing dogs. Then there are dogs that do not shed very much and therefore are not scattering dander around the house as easily as those who shed a lot. There are also dogs who have no coat at all, and their skin, if kept moist and healthy, will produce very little dander. But those dogs have another essence that is considered aggravating: oil. Certain oils in every dog's skin and coat are offensive to sensitive people. This, of course, is an easy fix with frequent bathing using a moisturizing shampoo. So, is there such a thing as a hypoallergenic dog? Of course! Maybe. Possibly.

Q. How is intelligence in a dog measured, and what is considered the most intelligent breed of dog?

A. There is a lot of controversy over this one. Dr. Lorraine says it's not a matter of any one breed being more intelligent than any other. All dogs are individuals. "You still have to look at single dogs," she insists. "That's like saying one race is more intelligent than another, or men are smarter than women. Some are, some aren't. It's really very much an individual thing with dogs." There are some who say that looking at the intent of the breed is a clue into their intelligence. The dogs that are bred to be working are bred to be more intelligent, because the working part is related to brain function. It thus stands to reason that the dogs in the working group may, as a group, be somewhat more intelligent than dogs in the toy group. But there are Toy Poodle owners who will argue this point until the cows come home. There's no way you can tell them that their little Muffy Poo is not every bit as smart as Canine Officer Rex down at the precinct.

There are intelligence tests that have been held up as the gold standard in determining a dog's overall intelligence. One such test involves tossing a small blanket or beach towel over your dog's head to see how long it takes him to come out from under it. Another test has you hiding kibble under an inverted cup and placing the cup beside two other cups. The dog has to figure out which cup hides the kibble and how to topple it to get at the food. But detractors say that these tests prove nothing, because they may be more about survival than intelligence. A while back, Stanley Coren published a list of the most intelligent breeds of dog in his book *The Intelligence of Dogs*. The top ten most intelligent, he writes, were (in order of their intelligence):

1. Border Collie
2. Poodle
3. German Shepherd Dog
4. Golden Retriever
5. Doberman Pinscher
6. Shetland Sheepdog
7. Labrador Retriever
8. Papillon
9. Rottweiler
10. Australian Cattle Dog

Coren theorizes that dogs possess one of three types of intelligence. The first involves learning and problem-solving abilities; he calls this "adaptive intelligence." The second is "instinctive intelligence," which he believes can be measured by standard IQ tests (some of which were described above). Finally, he discusses "working or obedient intelligence" which, he feels, is unique to the working breeds.

But it all boils down to what people look for in a dog. Some like dogs who are obedient, easily trained, and have an almost reverent view of their place in the world among humans. Some prefer dogs who are affectionate, loving, and gentle with kids. Others want a dog with athletic abilities or prowess in certain areas, such as hunting, swimming, or running.

And some want a dog they can just tie in the yard to scare away burglars. The irony is, the dog would happily run away with the burglar rather than stay with a person who would tie him up in the first place. And that would be one Smart dog!

Q. Can dogs blush?

A. Dog fanciers have lots of interesting, albeit useless, trivia at their fingertips at any given time. They whip out these unusual facts at parties and meetings in an effort to amaze and delight their friends. I suspect David Blaine started out by carrying a deck of cards everywhere he went for the same reason.

One of these little-known trivia tidbits is that the Pharaoh Hound is the only dog with the unique ability to blush. Described in ancient Egyptian literature as a dog whose "face glows like a God," the Pharaoh Hound's face and ears flush with blood whenever he gets excited. Dr. Lorraine is not so sure that the Pharaoh Hound is the only dog who can blush. "Maybe it's just the way their face and ears are structured. We can see it on the Pharaoh Hound because of his slender face, tall, thin, and vascular ears, and lack of thick facial fur; but we can't see it on other dogs. I know that dogs can be embarrassed.

I have seen a dog fall off the bed, and then look around with that guilty look on his face to see if anyone was watching. It's not an aggressive look, as if they thought someone pushed them; it's more of a submissive look, a look that says 'I'm embarrassed.' If the Pharaoh Hound is blushing in those situations I would say then yes, they are blushing. I would assume that all dogs do that and you just can't see it with the others."

Blushing, she explained, involves the dilation of blood vessels in the face, so we redden. It's related to making yourself look more dangerous to others, and could be part of the original fight-or-flight response. You are getting ready to run, so you are vasodilating. It's one of those things that had a purpose at one time, and we lost the purpose behind it. It could also be a sexual response. Color makes us more attractive; other animals use it all the time. Witness the peacock and certain other birds and fish who use color to attract mates. Humans do it too when they apply makeup. But are Pharaoh Hounds the only dogs who blush? Probably not. It's probably more related to a combination of their temperament and body style. They are dogs who blush when they are excited, and because of their pigment and other factors, it shows more clearly in their ears, face, and nose. Chow Chows and Collies probably do it too, though we'd never see it under all that fur.

Q. What purpose did small-breed "lap dogs" serve for royalty and the elite?

A. These dogs were held by the aristocrats to draw the fleas and ticks away from the humans. They were a sort of living, breathing bug zapper. This is especially true of the Cavalier King Charles Spaniel, who was bred specifically for this nefarious job.

FUR FACT

There is no such thing as a "thoroughbred dog." Thoroughbred refers to a specific breed of horse, like a Clydesdale or a quarter horse. The term used for a dog with two parents of the same breed is "purebred."

This is ironic when you consider that so many of the little breeds, such as the Pekingese, the Shih Tzu, and the Lhasa Apso were all thought by Buddhists to be dogs that held the departed spirits of loved ones, so their history is intertwined with Buddhist beliefs. This made them sacred entities and they were treated with a great deal of respect and reverence. The Pekingese, especially, was known as "the sleeve dog" because Chinese royalty would carry them in the large, pendulous sleeves of their garments. This was the forerunner of today's fad of carrying little dogs wearing diamond-studded collars around in chic purses, proving once again that everything old is new again.

Q. How did the Boxer get his name?

A. The Boxer has an unusual habit of hitting his opponent with his front feet, looking for all the world like a boxer in the ring. Where other dogs are more apt to use their teeth, mouths, and body slams, the Boxer stands tall on his back feet and flails away at his opponent. Dog boxers, however, unlike some human boxers, do not necessarily bite the ear of their opponents.

Q. Why is the Saint Bernard usually shown with a brandy flask around his neck?

A. I guess you could say the Saint Bernard is the original party animal, because he always showed up with the booze! Indeed, this dog's very countenance is so keenly intertwined with benevolence and love that meeting one with a bad temper is almost unheard of and therefore worthy of note.

The Monastery of St. Bernard is a hospice where the monks who first started breeding these dogs make their home. It is located in the Swiss Alps along a very dangerous passageway. Historical records show that the dogs were created by crossing the Tibetan Mastiff, Great Dane, and Great Pyrenees. These breeds were chosen for their strong, sturdy bodies; thick fur, which would shield them from the elements; and their fierce loyalty and willingness to please.

Hikers and others who made their way along the St. Bernard Pass would frequently become disoriented in flash snowstorms and avalanches and lose their way. If not found in time, they could easily die due to exposure to the elements. Saint Bernards would seek out those unfortunate hikers and stay with them, baying into the night to summon rescuers. The flask around the dog's neck contained brandy or other spirits of which the victim would partake to keep his warmth and courage up.

Q. Why do some dogs have floppy ears?

A. Today's pets are the result of careful breeding by people, rather than natural selection. Each dog breed once had a purpose for being brought into the world "just so." The dog breeds that have long, floppy ears are commonly called "scent hounds" and were used primarily for hunting. The Bassett Hound is an example of a dog with long pendulous, ears. The nice members of the South Florida Bassett Hound Club explained that the ears are extra long so that they can help pick up scents from the ground where they are tracking. These scents are gathered within the long ears and kept there so the dog can use his incredible sense of smell to assess those odors. The Standard Poodle, the Irish Setter, Bloodhound, Beagle, and many, many other breeds with long ears were all bred at one time to be hunters and/or trackers.

Scent hounds have more "stuff" near the nose. "Stuff" can be skin wrinkles or floppy ears. This tends to reduce air flow, thus concentrating the air for the sniffer to work. Makes sense!

Dogs with long, floppy ears come with a typical problem, however: yeast. Because the dog's ear canal is in a moist, dark, anaerobic (that is, without oxygen) environment, fungus grows prolifically. Dogs with erect ears are not as prone to that problem because the air circulates freely in and out of their ears, keeping them clean and dry. Other problems with long-eared breeds include stepping on their ears (in the case of a Bassett, because they are so low to the ground) and getting their ears in their water and food dish. This latter problem is alleviated by the use of a product called a "snood," a kind of hood that fits over the dog's ears to keep them from getting food and water on them. It looks a little bit like the hoodies that some rap stars wear, but it won't make your dog sing rhyming lyrics.

Q. Why do Pointers point?

A. This is a complicated question, but there is an explanation. Dogs were bred to perform specific tasks to help us in our day-to-day chores. Sometimes, as with hunting, those "chores" involve a predatory sequence of acts. First, they orient to the object or prey; this means they find it. Then, they stalk the prey; in essence, glare menacingly at it. Next, they give chase. Finally, they bring it down. Dogs bred for hunting have been bred over many decades in a way that inhibits some parts of the predatory sequence and supports other aspects. Pointers have been bred to inhibit all but the first act (orient/find or "point") in the predatory sequence and also bred for a strong inclination to do this part of the sequence. Pointers still need to be trained, but it is so much easier to train a Pointer to point than it is to get, say, a Poodle to do so. The dog will usually offer the behavior on his own, and the owner simply reinforces it with positive training techniques such as the clicker and a treat. A Pointer will hear the prey in the woods and point with his snout and tail in the direction of the prey, holding his paw up in order to exaggerate the arrowlike posture. The hunter will then aim the gun in alignment with the dog's nose.

So can a Pointer help you find the right car? The perfect mate? The winning lottery numbers? Probably not, but in this case, at least, it's not only polite to point, but essential.

Q. Which breed of dog makes the best family pet?

A. Ask any ten people this question and you will get ten different answers! But truly, the answer is that it all depends on the dog-seeking family. If your family is athletic, always on the go, and loves an energetic dog, then look to the herding breeds, such as the Collie, the Sheepdog, and the Australian Shepherd. If, however, yours is a family of couch potatoes, then you may want to look at the toy and miniature breeds. Though they can sometimes be hyperactive, they get plenty of exercise just "being." There are many great books and Web sites on breed selection to help you do your homework on this. Petfinder.com offers a resource for finding just the right dog as well as listings of dogs looking for homes. Sue Sternberg's *Successful Dog Adoption* and *Paws to Consider: Choosing the Right Dog for You and Your Family* by Brian Kilcommons and Sarah Wilson are two great books on the subject of choosing the best dog for your lifestyle.

When choosing a pet, remember that looks can be deceiving, and it's easy to make false assumptions. It may surprise you to know that retired racing Greyhounds make great pets for those with sedentary lifestyles, as they have been called the "forty-five-mile-per-hour couch potato."

But if the question is one of popularity, then the Labrador Retriever beats the rest paws down. According to the American Kennel Club, the Labrador Retriever is the most popular purebred dog in America and has been since 1990. The lab is followed by the Golden Retriever and the Yorkshire Terrier. The German Shepherd Dog and the Beagle round out the top five dogs in registration. Of course, there are those who would strongly argue that the best breed of dog for anyone is an American Natural Dog, otherwise known as "the mutt."

EPILOGUE

Whether it's ingrained, infused, instinct, or intelligence, dog behaviors and motivations continue to amaze and overwhelm us. We are filled with admiration at the way their bodies work and adapt. Their creativity in figuring things out so that they can relate to us and the world around them humbles us. So, no matter how much knowledge we continue to gain, I hope we never lose our curiosity and wonder about these amazing creatures. A little girl's simple question, "Do dogs have belly buttons?" is only just the beginning.

REVIEWER PANEL

Dr. Michael Berkenblit, DVM, was a research chemist for IBM before entering the veterinary school at University of California, Davis. He later taught at the veterinary school at Louisiana State University. He served on the weekly *Ask the Vet* television show on the West Palm Beach, Florida, NBC affiliate WPTV from 1995 to 2001. Dr. Berkenblit has served on the Palm Beach County Animal Appeals Board since 1996, and he and his wife, Dr. Lisa Degan, ACVIM, are co-owners of Village Animal Clinic. Dr. Berkenblit is cofounder and chairman of the board of Animals 101, Inc., a humane education project, and Pawsabilities Unleashed, a puppy training program at the Palm Beach County Stockade prison. He volunteers for numerous animal agencies, including Canine Companions for Independence and Greyhound Adoption.

Dr. Lorraine Kassarjian, DVM, grew up in Los Angeles, and worked for the U.S. Air Force as a mechanical engineer for six years and as an instructor at the Test Pilot School at Edwards Air Force Base. She later graduated from the Ohio State University veterinary school.

Dr. Lorraine now owns Jupiter Home Veterinary Services, a house-call veterinary service, and she is the vice president and cofounder of Luv-A-Pet Inc., a rescue for abandoned and orphaned puppies and kittens.

Susan K. Helmink holds a BS and MS in animal sciences from the University of Illinois at Urbana-Champaign, where she is a lecturer at the Department of Animal Sciences. Susan created and teaches Humane Education with Companion Animals, an undergraduate course taught within the Companion Animal program. She recently completed a five-year term as advisor to the Companion Animal Club, a registered student organization at the university. Susan is a Canine Good Citizen instructor, and she has been published in the *Journal of Animal Science*. Susan is a member of the Association of Professional Humane Educators, Association of Pet Dog Trainers, and many other animal-oriented organizations.

INDEX